*"Coming to Writing"*
*and Other Essays*

# "Coming to Writing" and Other Essays

## HÉLÈNE CIXOUS

With an introductory essay by
Susan Rubin Suleiman

Edited by Deborah Jenson

*Translated by*
Sarah Cornell
Deborah Jenson
Ann Liddle
Susan Sellers

*Harvard University Press*
*Cambridge, Massachusetts*
*London, England*
*1991*

# Contents

"Writing Past the Wall"
by Susan Rubin Suleiman   vii

1. Coming to Writing   1

2. Clarice Lispector: The Approach   59

3. Tancredi Continues   78

4. The Last Painting or the Portrait of God   104

5. By the Light of an Apple   132

6. The Author in Truth   136

"Coming to Reading Hélène Cixous"
by Deborah Jenson   183

Notes   197

Sources   208

Index   211

# Writing Past the Wall

## or the Passion According to H.C.

## by Susan Rubin Suleiman

> One cannot not speak of the scandals of an epoch. One cannot
> not espouse a cause. One cannot not be summoned by an
> obligation of fidelity.
>
> *Hélène Cixous, "From the Scene of the*
> *Unconscious to the Scene of History,"*
> *trans. Deborah Carpenter*

Ask any fashionable Parisian intellectual these days about
feminism or feminist theory—let alone, heaven help you,
"new French feminisms"—and you will meet with a pitying stare. "My dear, where have you been? Don't you know
that no one does that anymore?" Nothing is more embar-
rassing, to a fashionable Parisian intellectual, than to be
caught quoting last season's watchwords. Feminism, like
Marxism, structuralism, poststructuralism (or like the narrow striped tie?), is definitely *passé*. No one—that is, no
one fashionable, no one *dans le vent*, in the wind, knowing
which way the wind blows—"does" it anymore.

Ah, well, so much for *la mode*. Some of us may have to
resign ourselves to being unfashionable (at least for a while,
given fashion's fickleness), stubbornly clinging to what

matters to us, repeatedly returning to the same subject, which turns out to be inexhaustible, upon inspection never exactly the same; like Hokusai drawing his two hundred nineteenth lion, or Rembrandt painting his hundredth self-portrait, or Monet painting his twenty-sixth cathedral or *n*th water lily. Or like Hélène Cixous, who cites these examples in her meditation on repetition and fidelity, "The Last Painting or the Portrait of God."

What does H.C. stubbornly cling to? What is the "same subject" to which she keeps returning? The essays in this book, representing a tiny portion of her writing over the past fifteen years, provide a surprisingly accurate, if necessarily shorthand, answer to that question. But first we must slightly modify the question, for what these essays present is not a single subject but a whole web of intertwined concerns and reflections: on the relations between writing, exile, foreignness, loss, and death; on the relations between writing, giving, nourishment, love, and life; and on the relations between all of the above and being a woman—or a man.

These concerns have been H.C.'s ever since she published her first works of fiction and criticism in the 1960s (the title of her first critical book was itself an entire program: *The Exile of Joyce, or the Art of Replacement*); but they have become, over time, by dint of repetition and fidelity, reworked, refined, at once complicated and decanted—I would be tempted to say "purified," were that word not so heavily overlaid with spiritualist and antimaterialist connotations, many of which I do not accept. H.C.'s latest book as of this writing, *Jours de l'an*, published in 1990, takes up again, in a complicated and decanted way, the "author's" problem (the author is not named; the word acts as both a proper and a common noun, though in the feminine): the problem of death and loss, in childhood and later. H.C. has often said that she "entered into writing" when her father died, she a young child and he still a young man. In *Jours de l'an*, the anniversary of his death is linked to other losses, other deaths—but also to the author's necessary choice to live, and write; and to her "passion for doors" that will allow her to get to the "other side." Or as the title of one chapter puts it, her passion for "breaking down the wall."

## Walls

What exactly does it mean, in H.C.'s world and writing, to "break down the wall," or (in "Coming to Writing") to "get past the wall"? On an immediate, existential level, it means—as she explains in "Coming to Writing," the most explicitly autobiographical of these essays—daring to throw off the constraints, inner and outer, which join together to "forbid [one] to write." In H.C.'s case—but she is not the only one—the constraints were multiple: "History, my story, my origin, my sex." By what right did a "Jewoman" with a German mother(tongue), growing up in Algeria without a father, desire to enter the Sacred Garden of French Literature? No right at all, it seemed. But desire, like a breath struggling to get out after you have been held breathless, is precisely what does not ask whether it has a "right" to exist. The passion to write can even get past triple walls of interdiction, triple walls of difference: foreignness, Jewishness, femininity. "As soon as you let yourself be led beyond codes, your body filled with fear and with joy, the words diverge, you are no longer enclosed in the maps of social constructions, *you no longer walk between walls*, meanings flow" ("Coming to Writing," my emphasis).

Interestingly, H.C. reinvents here, in describing the process of a free-flowing writing that she associates with femininity, some of the vocabulary of early Surrealism. "Let yourself go, let the writing flow, . . . become the river, let everything go, open up, unwind, open the floodgates, let yourself roll"—this could be a recipe for automatic writing, the poetic mainstay of the first Surrealist Manifesto. Like automatic writing, H.C.'s practice is "at once a vocation and a technique," "a practice of the greatest passivity," which is actually "an active way—of getting to know things by letting ourselves be known by them." Cagey H.C., to rewrite the avant-garde by feminizing it! "Continuity, abundance, drift [*dérive*, a favorite word of the Situationists, inherited as a concept from the Surrealists, and passed on to poststructuralism via the writings of Jacques Derrida]— are these specifically feminine? I think so. And when a similar wave of writing surges forth from the body of a man, it's because in him femininity is not forbidden. Because he doesn't fantasize his sexuality around a faucet" ("Coming to Writing").

In other words, there is more than one way to get past a wall, and more than one kind of wall to get past. The wall of sexual difference, because it seems so impermeable, is one to which H.C. keeps returning. What fascinates her is precisely the imagined possibility of getting past that wall: "Is there a man who can be my mother? Is a maternal man a woman?" ("Coming to Writing"). "What interested me in Rossini's *Tancredi* . . . was the undeveloped mystery . . . of the existence of a character all the more man in that he is more woman, just as she is more man in that he is more woman" ("The Author in Truth"). Rossini wrote Tancredi's role for a female voice, woman singing as man; and he wrote Clorinda for a female voice, woman singing as a woman pretending to be a man. H.C. asks: "Where does man begin woman begin continue?" H.C. asks: "What do you call a person who looks rather more like a woman with dark blue eyes, an icy look in appearance, burning inside . . . , who fights like a hero, would give up her life like a mother, . . . and who takes fortresses more easily than a kiss, and her voice is so deep and warm and moist, it sounds like the sea of human tears . . .?" ("Tancredi Continues").

Is this poetry? Critical commentary? Autobiography? Ethical reflection? Feminist theory? Yes. One wall these texts most definitely get past is the wall of genres. Although H.C.'s formal Bibliography, published in an excellent recent volume of essays about her work, divides "novels, stories, and fictions" from "essays, theory, criticism," this division strikes me as purely arbitrary—certainly insofar as the works published over the past fifteen years are concerned.[1] The texts published here are all drawn from two books in the "essay" category; yet it is evident even on the most cursory reading that these are as much prose poems as critical or theoretical statements. And doesn't H.C. herself write, in "The Last Painting or the Portrait of God": "I am only a poet"? She means she is not a painter, only a "poor painter without canvas without brush without pal-

---

1. The Bibliography, prepared by Marguerite Sandré and Christa Stevens, is in *Hélène Cixous: Chemins d'une écriture*, ed. Françoise van Rossum-Guyon and Myriam Diaz-Diocaretz (Paris: Presses Universitaires de Vincennes, 1990).

ette." But still, she calls herself a poet, rather than, say, a writer or theorist. And some pages later she explains: "I call poet any writing being who sets out on this path, in quest of what I call the second innocence, the one that comes after knowing, the one that no longer knows, the one that knows how not to know" ("The Last Painting"). Baudelaire called poetry "l'enfance retrouvée à volonté," "childhood rediscovered at will." H.C.'s "second innocence," the innocence of knowing how not to know, is something akin to this Baudelairean idea. "It is not a question of not having understood anything, but of not letting oneself get locked into comprehension" ("The Author in Truth").

H.C. loves to cite Kafka's mysteriously beautiful sentence "Limonade es war alles so grenzenlos." Lemonade, everything was so infinite, so boundless (*grenze*: boundary). So wall-less. "De-nationalization is what interests me," says H.C. in a recent interview with Françoise van Rossum-Guyon. I ask: But why did K. say "lemonade"? What strange, impossible connection did he see between "lemonade" and "everything"? H.C., same interview: "Our richness is that we are composite beings."[2] Breaking down walls does not necessarily—not desirably—lead to oneness. Rather, it leads to the recognition of composite selves, composite tongues ("Blessing: my writing stems from two languages, at least"—"Coming to Writing"). Above all, it leads to the recognition of the stranger even in those one loves, or is.

---

2. Françoise van Rossum-Guyon, "A propos de *Manne*: Entretien avec Hélène Cixous," in *Hélène Cixous: Chemins d'une écriture*, pp. 222, 223. My translation.

## Clarices

Sometimes, when one is lucky, H.C. has said, one finds the *unhoped-for other*. "Two people came to speak to me in 1977 of a writer named Clarice Lispector. I had never heard of her, *Editions des femmes* [headed by Antoinette Fouque] was preparing a book of hers. I glanced at some fragments of texts, I was dazzled . . . And then as I went on in the text I discovered an immense writer, the equivalent for me of Kafka, with something more: this was a woman, writing as a woman. I discovered Kafka and it was a woman."[3] If Kafka had been a "Jewoman" living and writing in a language that was not her mother tongue, in a country that was not the country of her birth, he would have been Clarice. (Clarice Lispector was Jewish, born in the Ukraine, had emigrated to Brazil as a child, and wrote in Portuguese.) So, at least, thinks H.C. But who is H.C.? A "Jewoman" living and writing in a language that is not her mother('s) tongue, in a country that is not the country of her birth. Is finding the "unhoped-for other" but a way of finding one's other self?

Some painters, it seems, spend twenty years doing portraits of a single model. Thus the British painter Frank Auerbach: "To paint the same head over and over leads you to its unfamiliarity; eventually you get near the raw truth about it, *just as people only blurt out the raw truth in the middle of a family quarrel.*"[4] To see the most familiar face as unfa-

3. Hélène Cixous, "From the Scene of the Unconscious to the Scene of History," trans. Deborah W. Carpenter, in *The Future of Literary Theory*, ed. Ralph Cohen (New York: Routledge, 1989), p. 10.

4. Quoted in Robert Hughes, "The Art of Frank Auerbach," *New York Review of Books*, October 11, 1990, p. 28 (italics in text). It may be worth

miliar is to see it in its truth. Such seeing requires time and concentrated attention: painting the same head over and over. Above all, it requires a kind of love—which can also be, in a family quarrel, a kind of hate; but which cannot be indifferent, for to reach the raw, the irreducible, the unfamiliar truth about an other, one has to be willing to take risks. As H.C. puts it, glossing Rembrandt's self-portraits: "One must have gone a long way in order to finally leave behind our need to veil, or lie, or gild" ("The Last Painting"). To see and love the other in her or his ungilded truth, which is his or her unfamiliarity, one has to be willing to see, without flinching, the stranger in oneself. As H.C. puts it, glossing Clarice's fictions: "Who are you who are so strangely me?" ("The Author in Truth").

For more than ten years now, H.C. has been teaching and writing about Clarice, painting the same head over and over—nor is she finished yet.[5] We can get some sense of the ground covered in these years, these portraits, by comparing the first essay H.C. devoted to Clarice, "Clarice Lispector: The Approach" (1979), to the most recent one, "The Author in Truth" (1989). It's not that the first text is "less profound" or "less true" than the last, nor do they

noting that Frank Auerbach is himself a "displaced person," having left his native Berlin at age eight; his parents, who stayed behind, were both killed at Auschwitz (ibid., p. 28).

5. Clarice Lispector has been one of the authors treated in Hélène Cixous's seminar at the University of Paris for more than ten years. The other authors vary, and have included in recent years Isak Dinesen, Marina Tsvetaeva, Osip Mandelstam, as well as Rilke, Kafka, and Kleist, who are constant references in H.C.'s work. For a selection from the seminar in English, see Hélène Cixous, *Reading with Clarice Lispector* (Minneapolis: University of Minnesota Press, 1990).

present considerably different views of their subject. It's that in the last one there is more, and in more decanted form, of both H.C. and Clarice—two authors who are not one, but who are very close, very close; so close that in rereading Clarice's texts in order to understand the last work she wrote before she died (*The Hour of the Star*), H.C. is brought to reread, and rewrite, several of her own.

I am especially struck by the rewriting, in "The Author in Truth," of a story H.C. has often (re)written before: that of Eve and the apple. In one of her earliest versions, written before the encounter with Clarice, H.C. emphasizes irony and rebellion; her favorite character in that version is the "tall black serpent, all head and a tail covered with diamonds," whose beauty for her resides in his daring to break and defy the Law.[6] In the later version, "after Clarice," H.C. emphasizes not rebellion but pleasure; the character in the story who counts for her now is Eve, struggling to choose between the absent, abstract Law and the present, concrete apple. "Myself, I would have eaten it," says H.C. about another apple, which Monet renounced ("The Last Painting"). Eve likewise ate it, discovering "the inside of the apple, and [that] this inside is good. The Fable tells us how the genesis of 'femininity' goes by way of the mouth, through a certain oral pleasure, and through the nonfear of the inside" ("The Author in Truth").

Of course, it would be far too simple to suggest (as I may appear to have done with my "before" and "after") that

---

6. The early reading I am referring to is in *Souffles* (Paris: Editions des Femmes, 1975), pp. 180–181. I have discussed Cixous's "angry ironic" mode in chapters 2 and 7 of my book *Subversive Intent: Gender, Politics, and the Avant-Garde* (Cambridge, Mass.: Harvard University Press, 1990).

Clarice was the only, or even the most important, influence in what I see as one major development in H.C.'s mode of writing over the past fifteen years. I mean the development away from a mode of ironic feminist polemic—as in what is undoubtedly her best-known text, that brilliantly explosive and angry essay/manifesto/poem titled "The Laugh of the Medusa"—toward what I want to call a mode of lyrical feminine celebration. All these words should be in quotation marks, to indicate their tentativeness and my aversion to labels or strict categorizations. It is certainly not the case that in 1975 H.C. was all anger and irony, whereas in 1990 she is all mansuetude and lyricism. "Coming to Writing," which dates from 1977, is a text in point, astonishingly varied in tone and mode. But I believe there has definitely been a gradual shift in emphasis over the years, one that H.C., too, is aware of. "Ever since I left the heterosexual scene, I feel less anger," she told me when we talked about this in June 1989. Some of the texts in this volume (especially "Tancredi Continues," published in the same year as *Le Livre de Promethea*) are beautiful love letters to femininity, as well as to a living woman. But as the very names Tancredi (a man's name) and Promethea (a man's name modified) indicate, H.C.'s notion of the "feminine" and its relation to the "masculine," or for that matter of women and their relation to men or to other women, is not a simple one. For example, it is not just ("just") a question of the male body versus the female body. That may be one reason these love letters, written by a woman to a woman, can resonate so strongly even for a reader, man or woman, whose so-called sexual preference tends elsewhere. The "nostalgia for a happy love between two equal masculine and feminine forces," which H.C. sees embodied in Tancredi and Clorinda—and which, as she points out, is still feared as revolutionary—can take many different forms. And be embodied in more ways than one, or two.

That is where Clarice comes back in, after all. She comes back, that is, according to H.C. in "The Author in Truth": "The text [*The Passion According to G.H.*] teaches us that the most difficult thing to do is to arrive at the most extreme proximity while guarding against the trap of projection, of identification. The other must remain absolutely strange within the greatest possible proximity." Absolutely strange, yet as close to me as my own self. Which means, at the right distance: "Love your fellow being as if he were your stranger . . . Yes, Clarice's ultimate project is to make the other human subject appear equal—and this is positive —to the roach. Each to her own species."

We are rather far, here, from the question of "male/ female," or even of "masculine/feminine." Or rather, that question—which can never be ignored, or dismissed—has been subsumed (I stress: without being "swallowed up") into the question of self and other. That is why Clarice, when painted by H.C.—over and over—can become plu-ral, Kafka, Joyce, Rilke, Tsvetaeva, and all the others who are there without writing, each in her/his own species, at once familiar and absolutely strange.[7] That is why Clarice,

7. Besides those who are "there without writing," one might mention a number of important intellectual presences whose work and thought have made a huge difference for Hélène Cixous without being explicitly mentioned in her writing. Two who come immediately to mind are Antoinette Fouque, the founder of Editions des Femmes, who with a short interruption in the early 1980s has published all of Cixous's books over the past fifteen years; and Jacques Derrida, another native of Algeria (although he and Cixous did not know each other in Algiers, Derrida's native city, he has spoken with

as H.C. sees her, can even cease being a name and become a common noun. "Things of beauty come to us only by surprise. To please us. Twice as beautiful for surprising us, for being surprised. When no one is there to take them. It seems to us when they spring forth towards us that they are strokes of god; but when they come in we see by their smile that they are strokes of clarice."[8]

## Her Story, Our Story, History

Lúck: "I had the 'luck' to take my first steps in the blazing hotbed between two holocausts" ("Coming to Writing"). Is it possible for a European born before 1939 to think of history, let alone individual life story, as anything but a form of luck? Is it possible for any Jewish European born in that time to think otherwise? Frank Auerbach was sent away from Berlin by his parents in April 1939, a few days before his eighth birthday; he never saw them again. He was lucky, they were not. H.C. had the luck—without quotation marks—to be born to a German Jewish mother in 1937 not in Germany, but in Oran, Algeria. When Frank Auerbach sailed to England, H.C. was two years old. At three, she discovered what it meant to be Jewish: "My father was a military officer during the war (temporarily, because he was a doctor), so suddenly we were admitted to the only garden in Oran (Oran is a very desert city), that of the Officers' Club. But the place was a hotbed of anti-

affection about their common background), who has been a friend and major intellectual ally of hers for many years.

8. Hélène Cixous, *Vivre l'orange / To live the Orange*, bilingual edition (Paris: Editions des Femmes, 1979), p. 111. The English text is by Cixous, based on the translation by Ann Liddle and Sarah Cornell.

Semitism. I was three years old, I hadn't the slightest idea that I was Jewish. The other children started attacking me, and I didn't even know what it was to be Jewish, Catholic, and so on."[9]

Before the awareness of being a woman, there was the sense of foreignness: "People said, 'the French,' and I never thought I was French . . . I felt that I was neither from France nor from Algeria. And in fact, I was from neither."[10] At home, her mother and grandmother spoke German—it was her language of nursery rhymes and songs, later of poetry. But in school, it was a language of rules, intolerable; for H.C., it had to remain private and sung—English became the school-learned tongue. Before that, there were Arabic and Hebrew, both interrupted when her father died. In Algiers, where the family had moved after the war, they lived in an Arab neighborhood where her father had his practice. But "since I didn't belong to the European community and wasn't admitted into the Arab community, I

9. "Entretien avec Renée el Kaïm," unpublished manuscript (February 1985), pp. 4–5. All quotes from this text are quoted with the permission of Hélène Cixous; my translation.

10. Ibid., pp. 2–3. Cixous's father, born in Algeria, technically had the status of an overseas French citizen. His family had lived in Morocco before settling in Algeria, and like many other Sephardic Jewish families in the Middle East they still spoke Spanish at home; Cixous recalls, however, that he felt politically and culturally close to France during the 1930s, especially during the Popular Front government headed by the Socialists. Cixous's mother left Germany in 1933 after Hitler came to power, and was joined in Algeria in 1938 by her mother, who had lived in Alsace before World War I and was able to leave Germany thanks to her Franco-German passport. Many family members were deported, and perished in the concentration camps. Cixous's maternal grandfather, of Hungarian-Czech extraction, was killed on the Russian front in 1915. (Personal communication, October 22, 1990).

was between the two, which was extremely painful."[11] Many years later, in "Coming to Writing," she would sum it up: "No legitimate place, no land, no fatherland, no history of my own."

The miracle is that out of all this sense of lack, writing came. "At a certain moment for the person who has lost everything, whether that means a being or a country, language becomes the country. One enters the country of words."[12] Miraculous metamorphosis, when mourning becomes language, turns from emptiness to substance added to the world. "Exile makes one fall silent/earth [*taire/terre*]. But I don't want exile to make silence, I want it to make earth; I want exile, which is generally a producer of silence, extinction of voice, breathlessness, to produce its opposite."[13] *Taire/terre*, metamorphosis, wordplay. This is what another woman exile living and writing in Paris has called "transmuting into games what for some is a misfortune and for others an untouchable void."[14] H.C. says: "I lost Oran. Then I recovered it, white, gold, and dust for eternity in my memory and I never went back. In order to keep it. It became my writing."[15]

One aspect of H.C's recent work that is not represented, or even alluded to, in the essays in this volume is her writing of historical epics for the theater. She wrote two short plays in the 1970s, *Portrait of Dora* and *Le Nom d'Oedipe* (The Name/No of Oedipus), which came directly out of her

11. "Entretien avec Renée el Kaïm," p. 9.

12. "From the Scene of the Unconscious to the Scene of History," p. 5.

13. Van Rossum-Guyon, "A Propos de *Manne*," p. 215.

14. Julia Kristeva, *Etrangers à nous-mêmes* (Paris: Fayard, 1988), p. 58; my translation.

15. "From the Scene of the Unconscious to the Scene of History," p. 2.

involvement, at once angry and passionate, with psycho-
analysis. In the mid-1980s, she turned to a much vaster
stage. For Ariane Mnouchkine and her renowned troupe,
the Théâtre du Soleil, H.C. wrote two six-hour plays on
national epic themes: *L'Histoire terrible mais inachevée de
Norodom Sihanouk, roi du Cambodge* (The Terrible but Un-
finished History of Norodom Sihanouk, King of Cam-
bodia), staged in 1985, and *L'Indiade, ou l'Inde de leurs rêves*
(The Indiad, or the India of Their Dreams), staged in 1987
and televised in three two-hour segments in 1989. Also in
1989, H.C. and Ariane Mnouchkine collaborated on a tele-
vision film commissioned by the Ministry of Culture for
the bicentenary of the French Revolution. H.C. coauthored
the scenario and wrote the dialogues; A.M. coauthored the
scenario and directed. The film that resulted, *La Nuit mira-
culeuse* (The Night of Miracles), is a modern-day fairy tale,
at once poetic and full of comic touches, celebrating both
the Revolution (past) and cultural and national diversity
(present).

Although none of this work by H.C. is alluded to in the
present volume (most of the texts here were written earlier), all of this work is in some sense implied by it. For
breaking down walls and encountering Clarices will lead,
if not inevitably, still with a coherence all its own, to a
recognition of the other (of *others*) that is no longer limited
to individual life story. "It is when one has been able to
reach the moment of opening oneself completely to the
other that the scene of the other, which is more specifically
the scene of History, will be able to take place in a very vast
way."[16] For H.C., due to personal circumstances, writing

16. Ibid., p. 10.

the scene of History began literally with the "scene" of theater (*scène* in French also means "stage"). She has spoken with delight about the "depersonalization" of the author that writing for the stage both requires and makes possible, since the other in a stage production speaks necessarily with a voice different from the author's, and is physically someone else. But I believe that the scene of History, which she had already evoked, if only fleetingly, in "Coming to Writing," was waiting to make an appearance in H.C.'s work, in whatever genre or mode. Indeed, it appeared full force in her nontheatrical writing in 1988, with *Manne, aux Mandelstams aux Mandelas* (*Manna, to the Mandelstams, to the Mandelas*). In that book, exile, poetry, resistance, and fidelity—fidelity between a man and a woman (Nelson and Winnie, Osip and Nadejda, "two equal masculine and feminine forces") and between individual human beings and transhuman ideals—come together textually as part of the "blazing hotbed" of twentieth-century history.

Who has spoken here? A "Jewoman" living and writing in a language that is not her mother tongue, in a country that is not the country of her birth:   s.r.s.

*"Coming to Writing"*
*and Other Essays*

# 1

## *Coming to Writing*

In the beginning, I adored. What I adored was human. Not persons; not totalities, not defined and named beings. But signs. Flashes of being that glanced off me, kindling me. Lightning-like bursts that came to me: Look! I blazed up. And the sign withdrew. Vanished. While I burned on and consumed myself wholly. What had reached me, so powerfully cast from a human body, was Beauty: there was a face, with all the mysteries inscribed and preserved on it; I was before it, I sensed that there was a beyond, to which I did not have access, an unlimited place. The look incited me and also forbade me to enter; I was outside, in a state of animal watchfulness. A desire was seeking its home. I was that desire. I was the question. The question with this strange destiny: to seek, to pursue the answers that will appease it, that will annul it. What prompts it, animates it, makes it want to be asked, is the feeling that the other is there, so close, exists, so far away; the feeling that somewhere, in some part of the world, once it is through the door, there is the face that promises, the answer for which one continues to move onward, because of which one can never rest, for the love of which one holds back from renouncing, from giving in—to death. Yet what misfortune if the question should happen to meet *its* answer! Its end!

I adored the Face. The smile. The countenance of my day and night. The smile awed me, filled me with ecstasy. With terror. The world constructed, illuminated, annihilated by a quiver of this face. This face is not a metaphor. Face, space, structure. Scene of all the faces that give births to me, contain my lives. I read the face, I saw and contemplated it to the point of losing myself in it. How many faces to the face? More than one. Three, four, but always the only one, and the only one always more than one.

I *read* it: the face signified. And each sign pointed out a new path. To follow, in order to come closer to its meaning. The face whispered something to me, it spoke and called on me to speak, to uncode all the names surrounding it, evoking it, touching on it, making it appear. It made things visible and legible, as if it were understood that even if the light were to fade away, the things it had illuminated would not disappear, what it had fallen on would stay, not cease to be here, to glow, to offer itself up to the act of naming again.

The moment I came into life (I remember with undiminishing pain), I trembled: from the fear of separation, the dread of death. I saw death at work and guessed its constancy, the jealousy that wouldn't let anything escape it alive. I watched it wound, disfigure, paralyze, and massacre from the moment my eyes opened to seeing. I discovered that the Face was mortal, and that I would have to snatch it back at every moment from Nothingness. I didn't adore that-which-is-going-to-disappear; love isn't bound up for me in the condition of mortality. No. I loved. I was afraid. I am afraid. Because of my fear I reinforced love, I alerted all the forces of life, I armed love, with soul and words, to keep death from winning. Loving: keeping alive: naming.

The primitive face was my mother's. At will her face could give me sight, life, or take them away from me. In my passion for the first face, I had long awaited death in that corner. With the ferocity of a beast, I kept my mother within my sight. Bad move. On the chessboard, I brooded over the queen; and it was the king who was taken.

Writing: a way of leaving no space for death, of pushing back forgetfulness, of never letting oneself be surprised by the abyss. Of never becoming resigned, consoled; never turning over in bed to face the wall and drift asleep again as if nothing had happened; as if nothing could happen.

Maybe I've always written for no other reason than to win grace from this countenance. Because of disappearance. To confront perpetually the mystery of the there-not-there. The visible and the invisible. To fight against the law that says, "Thou shalt not make unto thee any graven image, nor any likeness of any thing that is in Heaven above or that is in the earth beneath, or that is in the water under the earth." Against the decree of blindness. I have often lost my sight; and I will never finish fashioning the graven image for myself. My writing watches. Eyes closed.

You want to have. You want everything. But having is forbidden to human beings. Having everything. And for woman, it's even forbidden to hope to have everything a human being can have. There are so many boundaries, and so many walls, and inside the walls, more walls. Bastions in which, one morning, I wake up condemned. Cities where I am isolated, quarantines, cages, "rest" homes. How often I've been there, my tombs, my corporeal dungeons, the earth abounds with places for my confinement. Body in solitary, soul in silence. My prison times: when I'm there, the sentence is of a really unforeseeable type and duration. But I feel, after all, "at home." What you can't have, what you can't touch, smell, caress, you should at least try to see. I want to see: everything. No Promised Land I won't reach someday. Seeing what you will (n)ever have. Maybe I have written to see; to have what I never would have had; so that having would be the privilege not of the hand that takes and encloses, of the gullet, of the gut; but of the hand that points out, of fingers that see, that design, from the tips of the fingers that transcribe by the sweet dictates of vision. From the point of view of the soul's eye: the eye of a womansoul.[1] From the point of view of the Absolute, in the proper sense of the word: separation.

Writing to touch with letters, with lips, with breath, to caress with the tongue, to lick with the soul, to taste the blood of the beloved body, of life in its remoteness; to saturate the distance with desire; in order to keep it from reading you.

Having? A having without limits, without restriction; but without any "deposit," a having that doesn't withhold or possess, a having–love that sustains itself with loving, in the blood-rapport. In this way, give yourself what you would want God-if-he-existed to give you.

Who can define what "having" means; where living happens; where pleasure is assured?

It's all there: where separation doesn't separate; where absence is animated, taken back from silence and stillness. In the assault of love on nothingness. My voice repels death; my death; your death; my voice is my other. I write and you are not dead. The other is safe if I write.

Writing is good: it's what never ends. The simplest, most secure other circulates inside me. Like blood: there's no lack of it. It can become impoverished. But you manufacture it and replenish it. In me is the word of blood, which will not cease before my end.

At first I really wrote to bar death. Because of a death. The cruelest kind, the kind that doesn't spare anything, the irreparable. It goes like this: you die in my absence. While Isolde is not there, Tristan turns to the wall and dies. What happens between that body and that wall, what doesn't happen, pierces me with pain and makes me write. Need for the Face: to get past the wall, to tear up the black sail. To see my loss with my own eyes; to look loss in the eye. I want to see the disappearance with my own eyes. What's intolerable is that death might not take place, that I may be robbed of it. That I may not be able to live it, take it in my arms, savor a last breath on its lips.

I write the encore. Still here, I write life. Life: what borders on death; right up against which I write my

## Letters from the Life-Watch: Who Goes There?

Stating, to lessen it, the fragility of life and the trembling of the thought that dares hope to grasp it; circling around the trap set out by life each time you ask the question death whispers to you, the diabolical question: "Why live? Why me?" As if it were a matter of death trying to understand life. This is the most dangerous question, as it threatens to arise, like a tombstone, only at the moment you have no "reason" to live. Living, being-alive, or rather not being open to death, means not finding yourself in the situation where this question becomes imminent. More specifically: we always live *without* reason; and living is just that, it's living without-reason, for nothing, at the mercy of time. This is nonreason, true madness, if you think about it. But we don't think about it. Once "thought" is introduced, once "reason" is brought into proximity with life, you have the makings of madness.

Writing prevents the question that attacks life from coming up. Don't ask yourself, "Why . . . ?" Everything trembles when the question of meaning strikes.

You are born; you live; everyone does it, with an animal force of blindness. Woe unto you if you want the human gaze, if you want to know what's happening to you.

Madwomen: the ones who are compelled to redo acts of birth every day. I think, "Nothing is a given for me." I wasn't born for once and for all. Writing, dreaming, delivering; being my own daughter of each day. The affirmation of an internal force that is capable of looking at life without dying of fear, and above all of looking at itself, as if you were simultaneously the other—indispensable to love— and nothing more nor less than me.

I'm afraid: that life will become foreign. That it will no longer be this nothing that makes immediate sense in my body, but instead, outside me, will surround me and beset me with Its question; that it will become the enigma, the irrational, the roll of the die; the final blow.

Terror: life arrest, death sentence:[2] every child's Terror. Perhaps being adult means no longer asking yourself where you come from, where you're going, who to be. Discarding the past, warding off the future? Putting history in place of yourself? Perhaps. But who is the woman spared by questioning? Don't you, you too, ask yourself: who am I, who will I have been, why-me, why-not-me? Don't you tremble with uncertainty? Aren't you, like me, constantly struggling not to fall into the trap? Which means you're in the trap already, because the fear of doubting is already the doubt that you fear. And why can't the question of why-am-I just leave me in peace? Why does it throw me off balance? What does it have to do with my woman-being? It's the social scene, I think, that constrains you to it; history that condemns you to it. If you want to grow, progress, stretch your soul, take infinite pleasure in your bodies, your goods, how will you position yourself to do so? You are, you too, a Jewoman, trifling, diminutive, mouse among the mouse people, assigned to the fear of the big bad cat. To the diaspora of your desires; to the intimate deserts. And if you grow, your desert likewise grows. If you come out of the hole, the world lets you know that there is no place for your kind in its nations.

"Why did you put me in the world if only for me to be lost in it?"

Determining whom to put this question to is beyond you.

Sometimes I think I began writing in order to make room for the wandering question that haunts my soul and hacks and saws at my body; to give it a place and time; to turn its sharp edge away from my flesh; to give, seek, touch, call, bring into the world a new being who won't restrain me, who won't drive me away, won't perish from very narrowness.

Because of the following dream:

My rejection of sickness as a weapon. There is a self that horrifies me. Isn't she dead yet? Done for. I fear her death. There, on that great bed. Sad, horribly so. Her sickness: cancer. A diseased hand. She herself is the sickness.[3] Will you save her by cutting off the hand? Overcome the atrocious, anguishing disgust, not at death but at the condemnation, the work of sickness. My whole being is convulsed. Tell her what must be said: "You have two hands. If one hand can't live, cut it off. You have twomorrow.[4] When one hand doesn't work, replace it with the other hand. Act. Respond. You've lost the hand that writes? Learn to write with the other hand." And with it-her-self-me-her-hand, I begin to trace on the paper. And now at once there unfurls a perfect calligraphy, as if she had always had this writing in that other hand. If you die, live.

With one hand, suffering, living, putting your finger on pain, loss. But there is the other hand: the one that writes.

## A Girl Is Being Killed[5]

In the beginning, I desired.
"What is it she wants?"
"To live. Just to live. And to hear myself say the name."
"Horrors! Cut out her tongue!"
"What's wrong with her?"
"She can't keep herself from flying!"[6]
"In that case, we have special cages."
Who is the Superuncle who hasn't prevented a girl from flying, the flight of the thief, who has not bound her, not bandaged the feet of his little darling, so that they might be exquisitely petite, who hasn't mummified her into prettiness?

## How Would I Have Written?

Wouldn't you first have needed the "right reasons" to write? The reasons, mysterious to me, that give you the "right" to write? But I didn't know them. I had only the "wrong" reason; it wasn't a reason, it was a passion, something shameful—and disturbing; one of those violent characteristics with which I was afflicted. I didn't "want" to write. How could I have "wanted" to? I hadn't strayed to the point of losing all measure of things. A mouse is not a prophet. I wouldn't have had the cheek to go claim my book from God on Mount Sinai, even if, as a mouse, I had found the energy to scamper up the mountain. No reasons at all. But there was madness. Writing was in the air around me. Always close, intoxicating, invisible, inaccessible. I undergo writing! It came to me abruptly. One day I was tracked down, besieged, taken. It captured me. I was seized. From where? I knew nothing about it. I've never known anything about it. From some bodily region. I don't know where. "Writing" seized me, gripped me, around the diaphragm, between the stomach and the chest, a blast dilated my lungs and I stopped breathing.

Suddenly I was filled with a turbulence that knocked the wind out of me and inspired me to wild acts. "Write." When I say "writing" seized me, it wasn't a sentence that had managed to seduce me, there was absolutely nothing written, not a letter, not a line. But in the depths of the flesh, the attack. Pushed. Not penetrated. Invested. Set in motion. The attack was imperious: "Write!" Even though I was only a meager anonymous mouse, I knew vividly the awful jolt that galvanizes the prophet, wakened in mid-life by an order from above. It's a force to make you cross oceans. Me, write? But I wasn't a prophet. An urge shook my body, changed my rhythms, tossed madly in my chest, made time unlivable for me. I was stormy. "Burst!" "You may speak!" And besides, whose voice is that? The Urge had the violence of a thunderclap. Who's striking me?

Who's attacking me from behind? And in my body the breath of a giant, but no sentences at all. Who's pushing me? Who's invading? Who's changing me into a monster? Into a mouse wanting to swell to the size of a prophet?

A joyful force. Not a god; it doesn't come from above. But from an inconceivable region, deep down inside me but unknown, as if there might exist somewhere in my body (which, from the outside, and from the point of view of a naturalist, is highly elastic, nervous, lively, thin, not without charm, firm muscles, pointed nose always quivering and damp, vibrating paws) another space, limitless; and there, in those zones which inhabit me and which I don't know how to live in, I feel them, I don't live them, they live me, gushing from the wellsprings of my souls, I don't see them but I feel them, it's incomprehensible but that's how it is. There are sources. That's the enigma. One morning, it all explodes. My body experiences, deep down inside, one of its panicky cosmic adventures. I have volcanoes on my lands. But no lava: what wants to flow is breath. And not just any old way. The breath "wants" a form.[7] "Write me!" One day it begs me, another day it threatens. "Are you going to write me or not?" It could have said: "Paint me." I tried. But the nature of its fury demanded the form that stops the least, that encloses the least, the body without a frame, without skin, without walls, the flesh that doesn't dry, doesn't stiffen, doesn't clot the wild blood that wants to stream through it—forever. "Let me through, or everything goes!"

What blackmail could have made me give in to this breath? Write? Me? Because it was so strong and furious, I loved and feared this breath. To be lifted up one morning, snatched off the ground, swung in the air. To be taken by surprise. To find in myself the possibility of the unexpected. To fall asleep a mouse and wake up an eagle! What delight! What terror. And I had nothing to do with it, I couldn't help it. And worse, each time the breathing seized me, the same misery was repeated: what began, in spite of myself, in exultation, proceeded, because of myself, in combat, and ended in downfall and desolation. Barely off the ground: "Hey! What are you doing up there? Is that any place for a mouse? For shame!" Shame overcame me. There is no lack on earth, so there was no lack in my personal spaces, of guardians of the law, their pockets filled with the "first stone" to hurl at flying mice. As for my internal guardian—whom I didn't call superego at the time—he was more rapid and accurate than all the others: he threw the stone at me before all the other-relatives, masters, prudent contemporaries, compliant and orderly peers—all the noncrazy and antimouse forces—had the chance to let fire. I was the "fastest gun." Fortunately! My shame settled the score without scandal. I was "saved."

Write? I didn't think of it. I dreamed of it constantly, but with the chagrin and the humility, the resignation and the innocence, of the poor. Writing is God. But it is not your God. Like the Revelation of a cathedral: I was born in a country where culture had returned to nature—had become flesh once again. Ruins that are not ruins, but hymns of luminous memory, Africa sung by the sea night and day. The past wasn't past. Just curled up like the prophet in the bosom of time. At the age of eighteen, I discovered "culture." The monument, its splendor, its menace, its *discourse*. "Admire me. I am the spirit of Christianity. Down on your knees, offspring of the bad race. Transient. I was erected for my followers. Out, little Jewess. Quick, before I baptize you." "Glory": what a word! A name for armies or cathedrals or lofty victories; it wasn't a word for Jewoman. Glory, stained-glass windows, flags, domes, constructions, masterpieces—how to avoid recognizing your beauty, keep it from reminding me of my foreignness?

One summer I get thrown out of the cathedral of Cologne. It's true that I had bare arms; or was it a bare head? A priest kicks me out. Naked. I felt naked for being Jewish, Jewish for being naked, naked for being a woman, Jewish for being flesh and joyful!—So I'll take all your books. But the cathedrals I'll leave behind. Their stone is sad and male.

The texts I ate, sucked, suckled, kissed. I am the innumerable child of their masses.

But write? With what right? After all, I read them without any right, without permission, without their knowledge.

The way I might have prayed in a cathedral, sending their God an impostor-message.

Write? I was dying of desire for it, of love, dying to give writing what it had given to me. What ambition! What impossible happiness. To nourish my own mother. Give her, in turn, my milk? Wild imprudence.

No need for a severe superego to prevent me from writing: nothing in me made such an act plausible or conceivable. How many workers' children dream of becoming Mozart or Shakespeare?

Everything in me joined forces to forbid me to write: History, my story, my origin, my sex. Everything that constituted my social and cultural self. To begin with the necessary, which I lacked, the material that writing is formed of and extracted from: language. You want—to Write? In what language? Property, rights, had always policed me: I learned to speak French in a garden from which I was on the verge of expulsion for being a Jew. I was of the race of Paradise-losers. Write French? With what right? Show us your credentials! What's the password? Cross yourself! Put out your hands, let's see those paws! What kind of nose is that?

I said "write French." One writes *in*. Penetration. Door. Knock before entering. Strictly forbidden.

"You are not from here. You are not at home here. Usurper!"

"It's true. No right. Only love."

Write? Taking pleasure as the gods who created the books take pleasure and give pleasure, *endlessly;* their bodies of paper and blood; their letters of flesh and tears; they put an end to the end. The human gods, who don't know what they've done; what their visions, their words, do to us. How could I have not wanted to write? When books took me, transported me, pierced me to the entrails, allowed me to feel their disinterested power; when I felt loved by a text that didn't address itself to me, or to you, but to the other; when I felt pierced through by life itself, which doesn't judge, or choose, which touches without designating; when I was agitated, torn out of myself, by love? When my being was populated, my body traversed and fertilized, how could I have closed myself up in silence? Come to me, I will come to you. When love makes love to you, how can you keep from murmuring, saying its names, giving thanks for its caresses?

You can desire. You can read, adore, be invaded. But writing is not granted to you. Writing is reserved for the chosen. It surely took place in a realm inaccessible to the small, to the humble, to women. In the intimacy of the sacred. Writing spoke to its prophets from a burning bush. But it must have been decided that bushes wouldn't dialogue with women.

Didn't experience prove it? I thought it addressed itself not to ordinary men, however, but only to the righteous, to beings fashioned out of separation, for solitude. It asked everything of them, took everything from them, it was merciless and tender, it dispossessed them entirely of all riches, all bonds, it lightened them, stripped them bare; then it granted them passage: toward the most distant, the nameless, the endless. It gave them leave—this was a right and a necessity. They would never arrive. They would never be found by the limit. It would be with them, in the future, like no one.

Thus, for this elite, the gorgeous journey without horizon, beyond everything, the appalling but intoxicating excursion toward the never-yet-said.

But for you, the tales announce a destiny of restriction and oblivion; the brevity, the lightness of a life that steps out of mother's house only to make three little detours that lead you back dazed to the house of your grandmother, for whom you'll amount to no more than a mouthful. For you, little girl, little jug of milk, little pot of honey, little basket, experience reveals it, history promises you this minute alimentary journey that brings you back quickly indeed to the bed of the jealous Wolf, your ever-insatiable grandmother, as if the law ordained that the mother should be constrained to sacrifice her daughter, to expiate the audacity of having relished the good things in life in the form of her pretty red offspring. Vocation of the swallowed up, voyage of the scybalum.

So for the sons of the Book: research, the desert, inexhaustible space, encouraging, discouraging, the march straight ahead. For the daughters of the housewife: the straying into the forest. Deceived, disappointed, but brimming with curiosity. Instead of the great enigmatic duel with the Sphinx, the dangerous questioning addressed to the body of the Wolf: What is the body for? Myths end up having our hides. Logos opens its great maw, and swallows us whole.

Speaking (crying out, yelling, tearing the air, rage drove me to this endlessly) doesn't leave traces: you can speak—it evaporates, ears are made for not hearing, voices get lost. But writing! Establishing a contract with time. Noting! Making yourself noticed!!!

"Now *that* is forbidden."

All the reasons I had for believing I didn't have the right to write, the good, the less good, and the really wrong reasons: I had no grounds from which to write. No legitimate place, no land, no fatherland, no history of my own.

Nothing falls to me by right—or rather everything does, and no more so to me than to any other.

"I have no roots: from what sources could I take in enough to nourish a text? Diaspora effect.

"I have no legitimate tongue. In German I sing; in English I disguise myself; in French I fly, I thieve. On what would I base a text?

"I am already so much the inscription of a divergence that a further divergence is impossible. They teach me the following lesson: you, outsider, fit in. Take the nationality of the country that tolerates you. Be good, return to the ranks, to the ordinary, the imperceptible, the domestic."

Here are your laws: you will not kill, you will be killed,

you will not steal, you will not be a bad recruit, you will not be sick or crazy (this would be a lack of consideration for your hosts), you will not zigzag. You will not write. You will learn to calculate. You will not touch. In whose name would I write?

You, write? But who do you think you are? Could I say: "It's not me, it's the breath!"? "No one." And this was true: I didn't think I was anyone.

This was in fact what most obscurely worried me and pained me: being no one. Everyone was someone, I felt, except me. I was no one. "Being" was reserved for those full, well-defined, scornful people who occupied the world with their assurance, took their places without hesitation, were at home everywhere where I "was"-n't except as an infraction, intruder, little scrap from elsewhere, always on the alert. The untroubled ones. "To be?" What self-confidence! I thought to myself: "I could have not been." And: "I will be." But to say "I am"? I who? Everything that designated me publicly, that I made use of—you don't turn down an oar when you're drifting—was misleading and false. I didn't deceive myself, but, objectively, I deceived the world. My true identification papers were false. I wasn't even a little girl, I was a fearful and wild animal, and I was ferocious (although they may have suspected this). Nationality? "French." Not my fault! *They* put me in the position of imposture. Even now, I sometimes feel pushed to explain myself, to excuse myself, to rectify, like an old reflex. For at least I believed, if not in the truth of being, in a rigor, a purity of language. If a given word turned to the practice of lying, it was because it was being mistreated. Twisted, abused, used idiotically.

"I am": who would dare to speak like God? Not

I . . . *What* I was, if that could be described, was a whirlwind of tensions, a series of fires, ten thousand scenes of violence (history had nourished me on this: I had the "luck" to take my first steps in the blazing hotbed between two holocausts, in the midst, in the very bosom of racism, to be three years old in 1940, to be Jewish, one part of me in the concentration camps, one part of me in the "colonies").

So all my lives are divided between two principal lives, my life up above and my life down below. Down below I claw, I am lacerated, I sob. Up above I pleasure. Down below, carnage, limbs, quarterings, tortured bodies, noises, engines, harrow. Up above, face, mouth, aura; torrent of the silence of the heart.

## Infantasies

("She first awakens at the touch of love; before this time she is a dream. Two stages, however, can be distinguished in this dream existence: in the first stage love dreams about her, in the second, she dreams about love.")[8]

## His Mouth

When I was three years old, God was an elegant and maternal young man, whose head, perhaps ceremonially hatted, soared into the clouds, and whose slim legs were sheathed in impeccably pleated pants. Not an athlete. Rather, a refined man with a vague chest, whose musculature was spiritual.

I lived in the left-hand pocket of his coat. Despite my tender age, I was his Pocket-Woman. As such, I didn't resemble myself, I was my opposite, svelte, fairy-like, petite, red-headed, clothed in a green dress. If I had come upon the idea of seduction, I would have pictured myself up there as seductive. I was, when I was living in the divine pocket, my other. From this position I began to look at the universe. I was happy. No one could reach us. As close as possible to the heart of God, to his middle and his lungs. His light gray suit. Never did I see his hands. I knew that he had a beautiful mouth. The lips of his Word: its pods of flesh with their neatly drawn contours. His mouth detached itself from his face, shone, distinguished itself. Thy mouth is a slice of pomegranate (I corrected the Bible).

Face: I lived it, received it. Primitive figure of a cosmos in which the dominant star, the sun, was the mouth. I didn't think of the eyes. I don't remember ever having seen or imagined the eyes of God. And God didn't flash withering looks: he smiled. He opened up.

And I went in and out of his breast pocket. The body of God was superior. Smile! In I go: mouse.[9]

Later I vaguely made him eyes like mouths. The lids had the engraving of the adored lips. Sometimes the lids fluttered and the eyes took sudden flight.

But the mouth of God advanced slowly, the lips parted and I lost myself in the contemplation of his teeth. Up above, I lived in the humid light of the teeth. His mouth, my hole, my temple; mouse, I go in and out between the teeth of the good lord cat.

My life down below, tumult and rage. As myself, I was a center of passions, fear and trembling, fury and vengeance. No precise form. All I knew of my body was the play of forces, not the play, the firing. Down below it was war. I was war. War and pleasure. Pleasure and despair. Power and feebleness. I watched, I kept vigil, I spied, I never closed my eyes, I saw the incessant work of death. Me: the lamb. Me: the wolf.

I beat up children. The Enemy's little ones. The little pedigreed French. Well-cut, well-dressed, well-planed, well-effaced, well-scrubbed, -nourished, -rubbed. Little pink and blue sugarplums filled with venom and shit on the inside. Little marionettes with little unmoving eyes carved out of hatred stupidity ferocity. I didn't dare put out their eyes. Or hang them. Too obvious. I was afraid. I committed my murders on the sly. One day in the Officers' Park, I killed a harmless little chick. Her innocence was unpardonable. She was three or four years old, I was five or six. She strolled along hopping and pecking in the flower-lined pathways. In her eyes were the reflections of flowers, mommy, missal, candy. No hate. Not a trace of a beggar, not a shadow of a slave, of an Arab, of wretchedness. Back and forth between the flowers the arms the sweet things. She dared to be unaltered. The ruse came to me. I lured her into a corner. I would play the Snow White trick on her. My weapon: the core of a pear on which I had left a few morsels of flesh. I initiated her: "It's a sweet. You have to swallow it whole." Pure, she would obey me, she would swallow, the core would not go down, she would choke. She was white, I was black.

I killed. I tortured. I struck, cheated, stole. In dreams. Sometimes in reality. Guilty? Yes. Not guilty? Yes. Colonized, I decolonized. Bit, ate, vomited up. And was punished, punished. Spanked. My curls shorn, my eyes put out.

I adored God my mother. Love me! Don't abandon me! He who abandons me is my mother. My father dies: thus father you are my mother. My mother remains. In me forever the fighting mother, the enemy of death. My father falls. In me, forever, the father is afraid, the mother resists.

Up above, I live in writing. I read to live. I began to read very early: I didn't eat, I read. I always "knew," without knowing it, that I nourished myself with texts. Without knowing it. Or without metaphor. There was little room for metaphor in my existence, a very confined space which I frequently nullified. I had two hungers: a good one and a bad one. Or the same one, suffered differently. Being hungry for books was my joy and my torture. I had almost no books. No money, no book. I gnawed through the municipal library in a year. I nibbled, and at the same time I devoured. As with the Hanukkah cakes: little annual treasure of ten cakes with cinnamon and ginger. How to conserve them while consuming them? Torture: desire and calculation. Economy of torment. Through the mouth I learned the cruelty of each decision, one single bite, the irreversible. Keeping and not enjoying. Enjoying and no longer enjoying. Writing is my father, my mother, my endangered nurse.

I was raised on the milk of words. Languages nourished me. I hated to eat what was on a plate. Dirty carrots, nasty soups, the aggression of forks and spoons. "Open your mouth." "No." I let myself be fed only by voice, by words. A deal was made: I would swallow only if I was given something to hear. Thirst of my ears. Blackmail for delights. While I was eating, incorporating, letting myself be force-fed, my head was enchanted, my thoughts escaped, my body here, my spirit on endless journeys. If I tasted anything, it was the stuff of speech. I remember, from the same period, the last bottle and the first book. I let go of one only for the other.

There is a language that I speak or that speaks (to) me in all tongues. A language at once unique and universal that resounds in each national tongue when a poet speaks it. In each tongue, there flows milk and honey. And this language I know, I don't need to enter it, it surges from me, it flows, it is the milk of love, the honey of my unconscious. The language that women speak when no one is there to correct them.

Perhaps I was able to write only because this language escaped the fate reserved for little red riding hoods. When you don't put your tongue in your pocket, there's always a gramma-r to censure it.

I had this luck, to be the daughter of the voice. Blessing: my writing stems from two languages, at least. In my tongue the "foreign" languages are my sources, my agitations. "Foreign": the music in me from elsewhere; precious warning: don't forget that all is not here, rejoice in being only a particle, a seed of chance, there is no center of the world, arise, behold the innumerable, listen to the untranslatable. Remember that everything is there; everything (which) is beyond everything. Languages pass into my tongue, understand one another, call to one another, touch and alter one another, tenderly, timidly, sensually; blend their personal pronouns together, in the effervescence of differences. Prevent "my language" from taking itself for my own; worry it and enchant it. Necessity, in the bosom of my language, for games and migrations of words, of letters, of sounds; my texts will never adequately tell its boons: the agitation that will not allow any law to impose itself; the opening that lets infinity pour out.

In the language I speak, the mother tongue resonates, tongue of my mother, less language than music, less syntax

than song of words, beautiful *Hochdeutsch,* throaty warmth
from the north in the cool speech of the south. Mother
German is the body that swims in the current, between my
tongue's borders, the maternal loversoul,[10] the wild tongue
that gives form to the oldest the youngest of passions, that
makes milky night in the French day. Isn't written: tra-
verses me, makes love to me, makes me love, speak, laugh
from feeling its air caressing my throat.

My German mother in my mouth, in my larynx,
rhythms me.

Horror the late day when I discovered that German can
also be written. Learning German as a "second language,"
as they say. Trying to make the primitive language, the
flesh of breath, into an object-tongue. *Ma lalemande!*[11] My
nourishment. To suddenly sheath it, corset it, lace it, spell
it! I fled, I spit it out, I vomited. I threw myself into
*languelait* at the intersection of the other languages, so as
not to see how the letters escort, laminate, extort, excoriate,
reappropriate the blood of the tongues between their paws,
their claws, and their teeth. The mother I speak has never
been subjected to the gramma-r wolf. In me she sings and
muses; my accent is right, but my voice is illiterate. It is she
who makes the French language always seem foreign to
me. To her, my untamed one, I am indebted for never
having had a rapport of mastery, of ownership with any
language; for having always been in the wrong, guilty of
fraud; for having always wanted to approach every language delicately, never as my own, in order to lick it, to
breathe it in, to adore its differences, respect its gifts, its
talents, its movements. Above all to keep it in the elsewhere
that carries it along, to leave its foreignness intact, not bring
it back to here, not deliver it to the blind violence of trans-

lation. If you do not possess a language, you can be possessed by it: let the tongue remain foreign to you. Love it like your fellow creature.

How could sexual difference not be troubled when, in my language, it's my father who is pregnant with my mother?

In French, carving out a pass: the door, the route, wanting to go ahead, to keep exceeding the language of a text; to break with it and to make it a point of departure; to confront culture, meaning, what is acquired; to not be spoken; to spar; to play; to make the repressed ones speak. In my womb, in my lungs, in my throat, the voices of foreign women give me pleasure, and it is the water of another sea-mother that comes to my mouth.

I beat my books: I caressed them. Page after page, O beloved, licked, lacerated. With nail marks all around the printed body. What pain you cause me! I read you, I adore you, I venerate you, I listen to your word, O burning bush, but you consume yourself! You're going to burn out! Stay! Don't abandon me. Blessing of the book: once the cakes were incorporated, I found myself empty, deceived, condemned again. A year to get through! (But a year, I've learned, is too long and is nothing. I learned all the subtleties of time very early, its elasticity in inflexibility, its meanness in compassion, its ability to return.)

The book—I could reread it with the help of memory and forgetting. Could begin again. From another perspective, from another and yet another. Reading, I discovered that writing is endless. Everlasting. Eternal.

Writing or God. God the writing. The writing God. I had only to break in and train my appetites.

I remember, at the age of twelve or thirteen, reading the following sentence: "The flesh is sad, alas, and I have read all the books."[12] I was struck with astonishment mingled with scorn and disgust. As if a tomb had spoken. What a lie! And beyond, what truth: for the flesh is a book. A body "read," finished? A book—a decaying carcass? Stench and falsity. The flesh is writing, and writing is never read: it always remains to be read, studied, sought, invented.

Reading: writing the ten thousand pages of every page, bringing them to light. Grow and multiply and the page will multiply. But that means *reading:* making love to the text. It's the same spiritual exercise.

And against death, to embody tenderness, in its humblest and proudest forms; to be the fidelity of a bird for its other bird, to be the hen the chicks the smile of my mother like the sun saving the earth, to be the force of love, above all: the good force, which doesn't accept the causing of suffering. Oh! I am the army of love—to love, alas, one must first embody the fight; this was my first knowledge: that life is fragile and death holds the power. That life, occupied as it is with loving, hatching, watching, caressing, singing, is threatened by hatred and death, and must defend itself. And I learned my first lesson of pain in this contradiction that reality, itself nothing but division and contradiction, imposes as its law: love, wanting only to know life and peace, nourishing itself on milk and laughter, is forced to make war on war, to stare death in the face. I have been all the couples between whom abysses opened up, or rather I have been this two-bodied flesh that the jealousy of the world seeks to dismember, against which are pitted the dirty alliances of kings, laws, surly egos, families, accom-

plices, go-betweens, representatives of the Empire of Appropriation, of the worst kind of proprietorship,[13] the
mouthpiece of the "you are (what is) Mine," not Adam and
Eve who lose only the paradise of the blind, who are banished only from the point of view of the divine, who are
born at last, who emerge, who become: I was the couple
hacked apart, severed, condemned in its flesh for having
found out the secret of pleasure, because in its body Eros
marries masculine with feminine, because Juliette is loved
in Romeo more than the Law and the fathers, because Isolde
enters Tristan as his joy, his femininity, Tristan resists
castration in Isolde.

I was the enemy of death, but does that mean "being"
someone?

I was this ensemble, buffeted, tormented by the need to
act; but where, how? By the need to move ahead? Toward
what? Twisted, pushed, projected in opposing directions,
divided, hurled, forward—but in what direction? And if
there were no forward direction? No other Forward than,
ambiguously, that which had taken place beFore?[14]

Speaking from this space pervaded by restlessness, how
could I have said "I am?"

My tumults were at the very most concentrated under a
name, and not just any name! Cixous—itself a tumultuous,
indocile name. That, a "name"? This bizarre, barbarous
word, so poorly borne by the French tongue, this was "my"
"name." An impossible name. A name to put outside at
night. A name which no one ever knew how to spell and
which was me. It still is me. A bad name, I thought when
they turned it against me, flaying me by flaying it, one of
those foreign, unswallowable, unclassifiable words. I was
no one. But I could, in effect, be "Cixous," and the thousand

distortions that ingenuity or hateful malice, conscious or unconscious, never grew tired of finding for it. Thanks to this name, I knew very early that there was a carnal bond between name and body. And that its power is formidable because it manifests itself at the nearest point to the secrets of human life, through the letters.

They could give me a pain in the letter, in my letter. And on the skin of the possessed, they branded a letter. So I was no one; merely a body scored by thunderbolts and letters.

I could have been called Hélène; I would have been beautiful, and unique, the only one. But I was Cixous. As an enraged mouse. I was so far from Hélène, a name which had actually been innocently transmitted to me from a German great-grandmother. With Cixous, imbeciles (some of whom will doubtless recognize themselves) make "sous."[15] And other low-level capital. With such a name, how could one not have been concerned with letters? Not have sharp ears? Not have understood that a body is always a substance for inscription? That the flesh writes and is given to be read; and to be written.

But I was no one. And no one, I said to myself, doesn't write.

If there was at first a time when the Breath's outbursts tormented me less, in my earliest childhood, it was because I didn't as yet feel guilty about being no one, and because I had no need to be someone. I was *"das Kind,"* this child that we don't have the wisdom to let circulate in French. For this language swiftly assigns the newborn to one side or the other of gender. Here we are, leaning over the cradle. And asking, "Is it a girl?" No error, please! Pink or blue? Quick, the signs. Are you sure you put your sex on properly this morning? In other languages you are allowed to digress, and the child remains a kind of neuter, in reprieve from sexual decision. Which doesn't mean that the repression of femininity is less significant where German or English is spoken. It's different, it intervenes in other terms. But there remains something undecided, a space for the hesitation of subjectivity, in these languages. This is not unrelated, I think, to the fact that in these languages it was possible for romantic agitation to flourish, with its way of unnerving the world of Being with its phantoms, its doubles, its wandering Jews, its people without shadows, its unpeopled shadows and the infinite species of its hybrids and other not-selves, somewhat-selves, somewhat different. There must be some *Es* in order for difference, for the not-self, to circulate. As *Es,* when I was still *"das Mädchen,"* I must have written without fear. But that wasn't Writing if it was already the crises of Breath.

Who? I: Without-any-right.

I got my period—as late as possible. I would so much have liked to take myself for a "woman."

Was I a woman? I am challenging the entire History of women in reviving this question. A History made up of millions of singular stories, but traversed by the same questions, the same fears, the same uncertainties. The same hopes that only a little while ago harbored nothing but consent, resignation, or despair. Take myself for a woman? How so? Which one? I would have hated to "take" myself "for" a woman, if I had been taken for a woman.

They grab you by the breasts, they pluck your derrière, they stuff you in a pot, they sauté you with sperm, they grab you by the beak, they stick you in a house, they fatten you up on conjugal oil, they shut you up in your cage. And now, lay.

How difficult they make it for us to become women, when becoming poultry is what that really means!

How many deaths to cross, how many deserts, how many regions in flames and regions iced over, in order to give myself the right birth one day! And you, how many times did you die before being able to think, "I am a woman," without having this phrase signify, "Thus I serve?"

I died three or four times. And how many coffins have taken the place of a body for you during how many years of your existence? In how many frozen bodies has your soul shriveled up? You're thirty years old? Have you been born? We're born late sometimes. And what could have been a misfortune is our good luck. Woman is enigmatic, it seems. This is what the masters teach us. She is even, they say, enigma personified.

Enigma? How do you set about being that? Who has the secret? She does. She who? I wasn't Her. Nor a She, nor anyone.

My trial began:

"Do you know how to do what women know how to do?"

What do they know how to do, exactly?

"Knitting." "No—sewing." "No—making pastry." "No—making babies." But I . . . I know how to act like a baby. Does a child make babies? Create order, flatter the tastes, anticipate desires? No. Act like a woman? I don't know how. What does she know that I don't know? But to whom should this question be put?

My mother wasn't a "woman." She was my mother, she was the smile; she was the voice of my mother tongue, which wasn't French; to me she seemed rather like a young man, or like a young girl; besides, she was foreign; she was my daughter. Woman she was, in that she lacked cunning, spitefulness, money sense, the calculating ferocity of the world of men; in that she was disarmed. She made me wish that I were a man, a just one, like in the Bible—so that I could fight the bad ones, the males, the wily ones, the merchants, the exploiters. I was her knight. But I was sad. Being a man, even a just one, weighed on me. And I couldn't be a "feminine" woman. There are just wars. But how heavy the armor!

Write? But if I wrote "I," who would I be? I could pass for "I" in daily life without knowing anything more about it, but write without *knowing* I-*Who,* how could I have done that? I had no right. Wasn't writing the realm of the Truth? Isn't the Truth clear, distinct, and one? And I was blurry, several, simultaneous, impure. Give it up!

Aren't you the very demon of multiplicity? All the people I caught myself being instead of me, my un-nameables, my monsters, my hybrids, I exhorted them to silence.

You can't stay put, where do you write from? I frightened myself. My unhappy aptitudes for identification came out in the practice of fiction. In Books I became someone, I was "at home" there, I found my counterparts in poetry (there were some), I entered into alliances with my paper soulmates, I had brothers, equivalents, substitutes, I was myself their brother or their fraternal sister at will. And in reality, I wasn't capable of being a person? Just one, but very much me!

Worse still, I was threatened with metamorphosis. I could change color, events altered me, I grew bigger but more frequently shrank, and even while "growing" I had the impression I was getting smaller.

Now, I believed as one should in the principle of identity, of noncontradiction, of unity. For years I aspired to this divine homogeneity. I was there with my big pair of scissors, and as soon as I saw myself overlapping, snip, I cut, I adjusted, I reduced everything to a personage known as "a proper woman."

Write? "Yes, but mustn't one write from the point of view of God?" "Alas! So go on, renounce!"

I renounced. It subsided. Let itself be forgotten. My efforts were rewarded. I saw my domestic sanctity glimmering. I regrouped myself. Pollarded myself. I was on the verge of becoming one-self.

But, as I have since come to know, the repressed returns. Was it by chance that my Breath returned at these specific moments of my history, when I experienced death and birth? I never dreamed of it then. If it was chance, it just goes to show that chance does things well. And that there is an unconscious.

I give birth. I enjoy giving births. I enjoyed birthings— my mother is a midwife—I've always taken pleasure in watching a woman give birth. Giving birth "well." Leading her act, her passion, letting herself be led by it, pushing as one thinks, half carried away, half commanding the contraction, she merges herself with the uncontrollable, which she makes her own. Then, her glorious strength! Giving birth as one swims, exploiting the resistance of the flesh, of the sea, the work of the breath in which the notion of "mastery" is annulled, body after her own body, the woman follows herself, meets herself, marries herself. She is *there*. Entirely. Mobilized, and this is a matter of her own body, of the flesh of her flesh. At last! This time, of all times, she is hers, and if she wishes, she is not absent, she is not fleeing, she can take and give of herself to herself. It was in watching them *giving birth* (to themselves)[16] that I learned to love women, to sense and desire the power and the resources of femininity; to feel astonishment that such immensity can be reabsorbed, covered up, in the ordinary. It wasn't the "mother" that I saw. The child is her affair. Not mine. It was the woman at the peak of her flesh, her pleasure, her force at last delivered, manifest. Her secret. And if you could see yourself, how could you help loving yourself? She gives birth. With the force of a lioness. Of a plant. Of a cosmogony. Of a woman. She has her source. She draws deeply. She releases. Laughing. And in the wake of the child, a squall of Breath! A longing for text! Confusion! What's come over her? A child! Paper! Intoxications! I'm brimming over! My breasts are overflowing! Milk. Ink. Nursing time. And me? I'm hungry, too. The milky taste of ink!

Writing: as if I had the urge to go on enjoying, to feel full, to push, to feel the force of my muscles, and my harmony, to be pregnant and at the same time to give myself the joys of parturition, the joys of both the mother and the child. To give birth to myself and to nurse myself, too. Life summons life. Pleasure seeks renewal. More! I didn't write. What was the point? The milk went to my head . . .

Another day, I have a child. This child is not a child. It was perhaps a plant, or an animal. I falter. Thus, everything happened as if what I had always imagined were reproduced in reality. Produced reality. At this point I discovered that I didn't know where the human begins. What is the difference between the human and the nonhuman? Between life and nonlife? Is there a "limit"? Words were pierced, their meaning fled. A breath is swallowed up. The child dies. Does not die. Impossible to mourn. A longing to write is everywhere. This is certainly perfect timing, I say to myself severely. I bring myself before the judge: "You want to produce a text when you are incapable of producing a child properly? First, you must take your test again."

"As a mother, one could do better. Are you aware of this?"

"Yes."

"Who are you?"

"I'm less and less certain. I give up."

The truth is, I have no "reason" to write. It's all because of this wind of madness.

And there's no help for it, short of violence and constraint. Impossible to forestall. The breath, what misfortune!

Are you going to shut up? They shut me up. Muzzle her. Silence her. Stop up her ears. I shut up. They examine me. There's something wrong with this organism. This beats too fast, that flows too hard. This heart is not normal. I'm sick, punish me.

"So," says the doctor, "we want to write?"

"A bit of a sore throat," I say, hoarse with fright.

He inspects me from head to foot, he cuts me up in little pieces, he finds my thighs too long and my breasts too small.

"Open your mouth, let's take a look."

I open my mouth, I say "Aah," I stick out my tongue. I have three of them. Three tongues? Pardon me. And what's more, he doesn't know that I have one or two that aren't attached there, or perhaps just one that changes and multi-plies, a blood tongue, a night tongue, a tongue that tra-verses my regions in every direction, that lights their ener-gies, urges them on and makes my secret horizons speak. Don't tell him, don't tell him. He'll cut out your tongues, he'll pluck out your teeth! "Open your eyes, pull in your tongue." I obey. The Master tells me: "Go to the city marketplace, describe it. If you reproduce it well, you will be given a writer's license." I don't get the license.

Every year a Superuncle tells me: "Before taking up the pen, tell me: do you know how to talk like a worker?"

"No."

"Do you really know who I am?"

"Oh yes," I say, "you are a capitalist-realist Superuncle. The Master of Repetition. The Anti-Other in papaperson."

He repeats his hundredth rescene for me: every year, it's the resame. "We think you're here. And you're there. One day we tell ourselves: this time we've got her, it's her for sure. This woman is in the bag. And we haven't finished pulling the purse strings when we see you come in through another door. Now really, who are you? If you're never the same, how do you expect people to recognize you? Besides, what's your principal name? The public wants to know what it's buying. The unknown just doesn't sell. Our cus-tomers demand simplicity. You're always full of doubles, we can't count on you, there is otherness in your sameness. Give us a homogeneous Cixous. You are requested to re-peat yourself. Nothing unexpected. A minimum of change for us. Halt! At ease. Repetition!

"As for the future, nobody's interested. Give us the same old reliable past. Above all, don't lead us astray. We've lived with your kind for five thousand years. Everyone knows what women are. Myself, I've had a wife, for thirty years."[17]

## Confession

I have an animale.[18] It's a nannymale, a species of meowse, a he- or she-bird, i.e., a miss-bird. It lives in me, it makes its nest, it makes my shame in its nest. It's crazy, it's edgy. I'm deeply chagrined to admit it: it gives me the greatest pleasure. Don't tell anyone. It's beastly.—Sometimes it's a dwarf, a very cunning Tom Thumb: seven leagues in one stride, barefoot—that's him. The animale is badly brought up, capricious and cumbersome. She comes when I call. When I don't call, she comes. She gets me into fixes. The Superuncle keeps tabs on me. He sneaks up with Wolf stealth, when I give it something to eat. Giving her pleasure is delicious to me, I don't hear the Wolf gnashing his teeth. The Superuncle howls, I jump in the air, my animale scrams. The old Wolf wants to separate us. For our own sake, for the right sake, for cunt's sake? He leans over the cradle, he hurls a curse at us: "If you bring her up, you will become more and more beastly. You will be crazy in the end. Men will have nothing to do with you. You will not become a woman."

What punishment! I am very afraid.

Chase her away! She comes back. She slips in between my thighs.

Her breathing is irresistible. Wild thing or woman?

With one hand she holds her animale pressed between her thighs, she caresses it briskly (as a "wild thing"). While with the other hand she does her utmost to kill it (as a man's "woman"). Happily, as ill luck would have it, beating it only adds to its joy. And me, my master, what will become of me? Wilder and wilder. Oh! I will never know. The nannymale carries me away, I am lost, ravished, I touch it, what am I?

Don't touch yourself. Run away from yourself. He will cut off your hand! He will chill your marrow. He will make you wear mitts.


## Requiemth Lecture on the Infeminitesimal

Gentlemen-gentlemen, Ladies-gentlemen,[19]

All the while I am preparing to worry you, I am ceaselessly struggling with your internal difficulties, and I feel in advance that I am in the wrong rightly, so to speak.

My writings really have no *raison d'être*. Folly, madness! In fact, I know nothing: I have nothing to write except what I don't know. I am writing to you with my eyes closed. But I know how to read with my eyes closed. To you, who have eyes with which not to read, I have nothing to reveal. Woman is one of the things that you are in no position to understand.

I've done everything possible to stifle it. What I'm saying is more than true. What's the point of sexcusing oneself? You can't just get rid of femininity. Femininity is inevitable. I ask you to take back your part of it. Take your shameful parts in hand. May Her proud parts come back to her.


The overfullness of femininity overwhelms you because you are men. But are you sure you're human?

To prove that I'm rightfully in the wrong, I've invoked all the reasons for the fact that I have no right to write within your Logic: nowhere to write from. No fatherland, no legitimate history. No certainties, no property.

No serious declared language. In German, I weep; in English, I play; in French, I fly, I am a thief. No permanent residence.[20]

No law. No grammar. Spelling once a month. No knowledge. Above all, no knowledge. Writing diplomas: none. Affiliations: none. Models: zero. The infinite.

## And Yet She Writes!

First she dies. Then she loves.

I am dead. There is an abyss. The leap. That *Someone* takes. Then, a gestation of self—in itself, atrocious. When the flesh tears, writhes, rips apart, decomposes, revives, recognizes itself as a newly born woman, there is a suffering that no text is gentle or powerful enough to accompany with a song. Which is why, while she's dying—then being born—silence.

I have nothing to say about my death. It has been too big for me up to now. In a sense, all my texts are "born" of it. Have fled from it. Are its issue. My writing has several origins, several breaths that blow life into it and carry it along.

Without it—my death—I wouldn't have written. Wouldn't have torn the veil from my throat. Wouldn't have uttered the ear-splitting cry, the cry that cleaves walls. What occurs during death is unspeakable. Writing is, in a certain sense (I don't believe I'm mistaken in thinking that there

are certain universal traits in our passage to death), first of
all the difference of a last sigh, of a phrase seized with terror;
and simultaneously already the headlong flight, the shudder
of horror—for in death we know the greatest, the most
repellent suffering—and the turning back again, the unspeakable, undisclosable nostalgia of what one has known
in this moment of marriage with death. What occurred
there is decisive, is absolutely unforgettable, but it remains
in a memory that is not our daily memory, a memory that
doesn't know, doesn't speak, that is only furrowed scarred
flesh; painful proof, but of what . . .

And from this period of death, one retains the greatest
fear and the greatest benefit: the desire to remain as close as
possible to Her, death, our most powerful mother, the one
who gives us the most violent push of desire to cross over,
to leap, since one cannot *stay close* to her, she desires and
incites desire; and this desire is split, it is simultaneously its
own opposite, the desire to approach her close enough to
die from it, almost, and to hold oneself extremely far back
from her, as far as possible. Because it is before her, against
her, right up against her, our most dangerous and generous
mother,[21] the one who gives us (although we aren't thinking, there isn't a glimmer of thought in us, only the tumult,
the roaring of blood, precosmic, embryonic confusion) the
staggering wish to come out, the desire for both extremes
to meet, enter into and reverse each other, and day doesn't
come after night, but struggles with it, embraces it, wounds
it, is wounded by it, and the black blood and the white
blood mingle; and in the same way, life emerges crawling
from the entrails of death that it has lacerated, that it hates,
that it adores, and it never forgets that death doesn't forget
it, that it is always there, never leaves it. open the window,

the terrible breast is there, the bed of peace—and this is life's greatest strength, it understands that death loves us as we love it, and that, in a strange way, we can truly count on it. That we move away from and approach Death, our double mother, through writing, because writing is always first a way of not being able to go through with mourning for death.

And I say: you must have been loved by death to be born and move on to writing. The condition on which beginning to write becomes necessary—(and)—possible: *losing everything,* having once lost everything. And this is not a thinkable "condition." You can't *want* to lose: if you want to, then there is *you* and *wanting,* there is nonloss. Writing—begins, without you, without I, without law, without knowing, without light, without hope, without bonds, without anyone close *to* you, for if world history goes on, you are not in it, you are "in" "hell," and hell is where I am not but where what is me, although I have no place, feels itself dying again through all time, where not-me drags me further and further from me, and where what is left of me is nothing more than suffering without myself, suffering uncircumscribed by self, for "me," left open, constantly feels the sense, the soul, the bodily and spiritual substances of the self streaming away, me empties itself, and yet, heavier and heavier, you sink down, you bottom-out in the abyss of nonrapport.

And so when you have lost everything, no more roads, no direction, no fixed signs, no ground, no thoughts able to resist other thoughts, when you are lost, beside yourself, and you continue getting lost, when you become the panicky movement of getting lost, then, that's when, where you are unwoven weft, flesh that lets strangeness come through, defenseless being, without resistance, without batten, without skin, inundated with otherness, it's in these breathless times that writings traverse you, songs of an unheard-of purity flow through you, addressed to no one, they well up, surge forth, from the throats of your unknown inhabitants, these are the cries that death and life hurl in their combat.

And this tissue from which your pains tailor this body without any borders, this endless wasteland, this ravaged space, your ruined states, without armies, without mastery, without ramparts—you didn't know that they were the gardens of love. Not demand. You are not jealousy, not calculation and envy, because you are lost. You are not in touch. You are detachment. You do not beg. You lack nothing. You are beyond lack: But you wander stripped down, undefined, at the mercy of the Other. And if Love comes along, it can find in you the unlimited space, the place without end that is necessary and favorable to it. Only when you are lost can love find itself in you without losing its way.

Now if you are a woman, you are always nearer to and farther from loss than a man is. More and less capable of loss. More attracted, more repulsed. More seduced, more forbidden. The same shadowy impulse, divided in direction, and always its own reverse, pushes you, restraining you, to lose.

For "woman," well imprinted with the sociocultural heritage, has been inculcated with the spirit of "restraint." She is in fact "restraint" itself, socially. (Or, if you wish, the repressed, the controlled one.)[22] She restrains herself, and is restrained, by a thousand bonds, hitched, conjugated, strings, chains, nets, leash, feeding dish, network of servile, reassuring dependencies. She is defined by her connections, *wife of,* as she was daughter of, from hand to hand, from bed to niche, from niche to household, woman as the complement-of-a-name has much to do to cut free. They have taught you to be afraid of the abyss, of the infinite, which is nonetheless more familiar to you than it is to man. Don't go near the abyss! If she should discover its (her) force! If she should, suddenly, take pleasure in, profit from its immensity! If she should take the leap! And fall not like a stone, but like a bird. If she should discover herself to be a swimmer of the unlimited!

Let yourself go! Let go of everything! Lose everything! Take to the air. Take to the open sea. Take to letters. Listen: nothing is found. Nothing is lost. Everything remains to be sought. Go, fly, swim, bound, descend, cross, love the unknown, love the uncertain, love what has not yet been seen, love no one, whom you are, whom you will be, leave yourself, shrug off the old lies, *dare what you don't dare,* it is there that you will take pleasure, never make your here anywhere but *there,* and rejoice, rejoice in the terror, follow it where you're afraid to go, go ahead, take the plunge, you're on the right trail! Listen: you owe nothing to the past, you owe nothing to the law. *Gain* your freedom: get rid of everything, vomit up everything, give up everything. Give up absolutely everything, do you hear me? *All of it!* Give up your goods. Done? Don't keep anything; whatever you value, give it up. Are you with me? Search yourself, seek out the shattered, the multiple I, that you will be still further on, and emerge from one self, shed the old body, shake off the Law. Let it fall with all its weight, and you, take off, don't turn back: it's not worth it, there's nothing behind you, everything is yet to come.

One can emerge from death, I believe, only with an irrepressible burst of laughter. I laughed. I sat down at the top of a ladder whose rungs were covered with stained feathers, vestiges of defeated angels, very high above the rivers of Babylon that twisted between the lips of the Land that is always promised. And I laughed. I was doubled over laughing. I was perfectly alone. And there was nothing around me. Nothing held me, I held on to nothing, I could move on without alighting, there was no road, in my left hand my deaths, in my right hand my possible lives. If there was godliness, I was of it.

I didn't seek: I was the search.

In the beginning, there can be only dying, the abyss, the first laugh.

After that, you don't know. It's life that decides. Its terrible power of invention, which surpasses us. Our life anticipates us. Always ahead of you by a height, a desire, the good abyss, the one that suggests to you: "Leap and pass into infinity." Write! What? Take to the wind, take to writing, form one body with the letters. Live! Risk: those who risk nothing gain nothing, risk and you no longer risk anything.

In the beginning, there is an end. Don't be afraid: it's your death that is dying. Then: all the beginnings.

When you have come to the end, only then can Beginning come to you.

At first I laughed, I cried out, a deep pain dictated my first letters from hell. Fashioned new ears for me for the future, and I heard the cries of the world, the rages and the appeals of the peoples, the bodily songs, the music of tortures and the music of ecstasies. I'm listening.

But if space without bounds hadn't been given to me

then, I wouldn't have written what I can hear. Because I write for, I write from, I start writing from: Love. I write out of love. Writing, loving: inseparable. Writing is a gesture of love. *The Gesture*.

Everyone is nourished and augmented by the other. Just as one is not without the other, so Writing and Loving are lovers and unfold only in each other's embrace, in seeking, in writing, in loving each other. Writing: making love to Love. Writing with love, loving with writing. Love opens up the body without which Writing becomes atrophied. For Love, the words become loved and read flesh, multiplied into all the bodies and texts that love bears and awaits from love. Text: not a detour, but the flesh at work in a labor of love.

Not the operations of sublimation. She doesn't give herself, in the text, derived satisfactions. She doesn't transform her desires into art objects, her solitude and her sorrows into priced products. No reappropriation.

Love can't be exchanged for social adaptation, its life signs have no market equivalents. Nor are the objects of dreams sublime objects. And like texts, they don't fail to affect waking life, they transform it, her life is more than diurnal: it is a life with many lives, all her night lives and all her lives of poetry. Thus, love extends and seeks itself, literally, carnally. If you write as a woman, you know this as I do: you write to give the body its Books of the Future because Love dictates your new geneses to you. Not to fill in the abyss, but to love yourself right to the bottom of your abysses. To know, not to avoid. Not to surmount; to explore, dive down, visit. There, where you write, everything grows, your body unfurls, your skin recounts its hitherto silent legends.

Love made a gesture, two years ago, a fluttering of eye-
lids and the text rises forth; there is this gesture, the text
surges from it. There is this text and the body takes new
flight. Read me—lick me, write love to me. She doesn't
put herself in the abyss to saturate the feared gapingness;
she celebrates her abysses, she wants them wide open, she
desires their bottomlessness, their promise: never will you
fill us in, you will never lack the good vertigo; for your
hunger, our sexes without end, our differences.

The text is always written under the sweet pressure of
love. My only torment, my only fear, is of failing to write
as high up as the Other, my only chagrin is of failing to
write as beautifully as Love. The text always comes to me
in connection with the Source. If the source were dammed
up, I would not write. And the source is given to me. It is
not me. One cannot be one's own source. Source: always
there. Always the vividness of the being who gives me the
There.[23] Which I can't stop searching for; I seek it furiously
with all my forces and with all my senses. Source that gives
the meaning and the impulse to all the other sources, illuminates History for me, brings to life all the scenes of the
real, and gives me my births every day. It opens the earth
for me and I spring forth. It opens my body, and writing
springs forth. The beloved, the one who is there, the one
who is always there, the one who is never exhausted, the
one who never runs out, but whose every phrase calls forth
a book—and whose every breath inaugurates a song in my
breast, a there that doesn't disappear although I don't "find"
it or enclose it, I don't "comprehend" it, a limitlessness, for
my limitlessness, the being that gives itself—to be sought
out—that prompts and relaunches the movement that
makes my heart throb, that makes me take up the ink and

go off again to seek farther, questioning eternity, untiring, insatiable, answer that poses a question, without end.

Love gives me the space and the desire for endlessness. Ten thousand lives don't cover a single page of it. What misfortune! What a blessing! My littleness, what luck! Not knowing the limit! Being in touch with the more-than-me! Gives me the strength to want all the mysteries, to love them, to love the threat in them, the disturbing strangeness. Love reaches me. Its face: its thousands of new faces.

Its look, the same Eternal One, and yet I had never received it before. Its voice, how to hear it, how with my human ears to hear the voice that makes ten thousand voices resound. I am struck. I am touched. Here. Here-There. My body is hit. Agitated. Under the blows of love I catch fire, I take to the air, I burst into letters. It's not that I don't resist. It speaks, and I am what is uttered.

Who makes me write, moan, sing, dare? Who gives me the body that is never afraid of fear? Who writes me? Who makes my life into the carnal field of an uprising of texts? Life in person. For a long time now, the names that are only right for the urge to possess have not been right for naming the being who equals life. All the names of Life suit it, all the names put together don't suffice to designate it. When I have finished writing, when we have returned to the air of the song that we are, the body of texts that we will have made for ourselves will be one of its names among so many others.

Neither father nor mother, nor brother nor man nor sister, but the being that love proposes we should become at that moment because it pleases us or is important to us in this scene, in these arms, on this street, in the heart of this battle, in the hollow of this bed, in this protest, on this

earth, in this space—marked with political and cultural
signs, and permeated with signs of love. Often you are my
mother as a young man, and I am often your daughter son,
your mineral mother, and you my wild father, my animal
brother. There are possibilities that have never yet come to
light. Others, entirely unforeseen, that have come over us
only once. Flowers, animals, engines, grandmothers, trees,
rivers, we are traversed, changed, surprised.

Writing: first I am touched, caressed, wounded; then I
try to discover the secret of this touch to extend it, celebrate
it, and transform it into another caress.

Is day hidden yet? At night, tongues are loosened, books
open and reveal themselves; what I can't do, my dreams do
for me. For a long time I felt guilty: for having an unconscious. I used to imagine Writing as the result of the work
of a scholar, of a master of Lights and measures. And you?
Myself, I experienced it by surprise, I didn't move forward,
I was pushed. I didn't earn my book by the sweat of my
brow, I received it. Worse still: I stole. I was tempted: there
was this garden without bars within which bubbled up all
the texts, a thousand and one tales a night. The fruits of the
Tree of Birth! My mouth watered! The tree of fiction!
Don't taste! It's only a dream! He who tastes of the fruit of
this tree no longer knows which side to wake up on. Every
night, forests of texts, tables laden with fantastic letters.
How could you resist? All this forbidden writing?

I stole. Timidly at first: not even a dream, not even a
piece of fruit, just its scent, a color, an ache, which I didn't
turn over to oblivion, which I retained, and whose vividness like a magnet at dawn, in the shadows of daybreak,
enabled me to attract a few fascinated phrases. "How do

they write?" I wondered, and my dreams went to my head. "What do they know, the wise men, the masters, the vanquishers of codes?" And there I was, hounded by dreams, flooded with visions, squelching about in unsubdued languages, I skirted the walls of their French parks with my abundance, my drunken lands, my wild orchards. And I didn't know how to draw a straight line.

On the sly, I stole myself. Don't repeat it!

These pearls, these diamonds, these signifiers that flash with a thousand meanings, I admit it, I have often filched them from my unconscious. The jewelry box. We all know what that is. Every woman has one. But sometimes it's empty. Sometimes she has lost the key. Sometimes it's papamama who has pinched it from her. Sometimes she can't remember where she put it away. Furtively, I arrive, a little break-in, just once, I rummage, ah! the secrets! (Note that in Henry James's *Aspern Papers* everything is there in the drawer, *on the condition that,* so that, the letters will be stolen.) I sneak a look, my hand follows suit. It's irresistible.

False signatures you're using there, I told myself not long ago.

"Thief!" "Me, a thief? But who's being 'robbed'?"

What belongs to whom? Whose love-pirate am I?

I listen to and repeat what women tell me at night. One part of the text comes from me. One part is torn from the body of the peoples; one part is anonymous, one part is my brother. Each part is a whole that I desire, a greater life that I envy and admire, that adds its blood to my own blood. In me there is always someone who is greater than I, someone nobler, someone more powerful, who pushes me to grow, whom I love, whom I don't seek to equal, a body, a soul, a text—human, whom I don't want to restrain, whom I want to let circulate freely, to whom I relish having to give the infinite. Hélène Cixous isn't me but those who are sung in my text, because their lives, their pains, their force, demand that it resound.

At night I gather up my body, I step behind the wheel, I slip between my curtains, I circulate between two blood-streams, according to what day of night it is I soar up, I descend, cities emerge from me, I travel through them, I leave them behind, all my outings on high. Am I dreaming? No. These are my lives that come to me, all the ones that lead me everywhere, into the regions, lands, countrysides, cities, cultures, nations, where my being has been touched, a single time suffices, to the quick, struck for life—to all the places from which a love letter or poison-pen letter has been mailed and then received so powerfully by my body that it could not not respond. They have led me into almost all the single countries, the compound countries, the de-composed or reconstituted countries—to all the sites where History has fertilized my geography. I travel: where people suffer, where they fight, where they escape, where they enjoy, my body is suddenly there.

Worldwide my unconscious, worldwide my body. What happens outside happens inside. I myself am the earth, everything that happens, the lives that live me in my differ-ent forms, the voyage, the voyager, the body of travel and the spirit of travel, and all of this with such suppleness that I go in and out, in and out, I am in my body and my body is in me, I envelop myself and contain myself, we might be afraid of getting lost but it never happens, one of my lives always brings me back to solid body.[24]

The tears I shed at night! The waters of the world flow from my eyes, I wash my peoples in my despair, I bathe them, I lick them with my love, I go to the banks of the Niles to gather back the peoples abandoned in cradles of reeds, for the fate of the living I have the untiring love of a mother, that is why I am everywhere, my cosmic womb, I work on my worldwide unconscious, I throw death out, it comes back, we begin again, I am pregnant with beginnings. Yes, at night love makes me a mother, I've known that a long time, I was already a mother when I had the taste of a last bottle still on my tongue. I was the mother of my mother then, of my brother, my whole family, I took them in my arms, I carried them over the hills, I saved them from the Nazis. Since then I've invented all different kinds of transportation, known and unknown. I've made planes that take off with a beat of the heart, I've laughed while reading da Vinci, one of my oldest young brothers, a feminine plural like me, I've been all the birds, joy of my life, the day it came home to me that my father was a stork. As a mother, I naturally needed wings. Carrier, ravisher, the one who lifts up. What I know today, if I didn't know it yesterday, because I wasn't watching myself, was already there. Flee, protect, escape, fly. Are you being pursued? Is censure is after you? Its chain of cops, pimps, misers, repressed types, edictators, ultraprofs, bosses, helmeted phalluses? How would you survive that armed bestiality, Power, if you didn't always have for yourself, with yourself, in yourself, a bit of the mother to remind you that evil doesn't always win out; if there weren't always a bit of the mother to give you peace, to keep a little of the milk of life through the ages and wars, a little of the soul's pleasure that regenerates? A taste of books, a taste of letters, to revive you?

So this is why, how, who, what, I write: milk. Strong nourishment. The gift without return. Writing, too, is milk. I nourish. And like all those who nourish, I am nourished. A smile nourishes me. Mother I am daughter: if you smile at me, you nourish me, I am your daughter. Goodnesses of good exchanges.

Mystery of hatred, of spite: isn't the one who hates devoured alive by hatred? Whoever keeps wealth and nourishment for himself is poisoned. Mystery of the gift: the poison-gift: if you give, you receive. What you don't give, the antigift, turns back against you and rots you.

The more you give, the more you take pleasure. How could it be that they don't know that?

I write "mother." What is the connection between mother and woman, daughter? I write "woman." What is the difference? This is what my body teaches me: first of all, be wary of names; they are nothing but social tools, rigid concepts, little cages of meaning assigned, as you know, to keep us from getting mixed up with each other, without which the Society of Cacapitalist Siphoning would collapse. But, my friend, take the time to unname yourself for a moment. Haven't you been the father of your sister? Haven't you, as a wife, been the husband of your spouse, and perhaps the brother of your brother, or hasn't your brother been your big sister? I emerged from names rather late, personally. I believed—up to the day that writing came to my lips—in Father, Husband, Family; and I paid dearly for it in the flesh.[25] Writing and traversing names are the same necessary gesture: as soon as Eurydice calls Orpheus down to the depths where beings change, Orpheus perceives that he is himself (in) Eurydice. As soon as you let yourself be led beyond codes, your body filled with fear and with joy, the words diverge, you are no longer enclosed in the maps of social constructions, you no longer walk between walls, meanings flow, the world of railways explodes, the air circulates, desires shatter images, passions are no longer chained to genealogies, life is no longer nailed down to generational time, love is no longer shunted off on the course decided upon by the administration of public alliances. And you are returned to your innocences, your possibilities, the abundance of your intensities. Now, listen to what your body hadn't dared let surface.

Mine tells me: I am the daughter of milk and honey. If you give me the breast, I am your child, without ceasing to be mother to those that I nourish, and you are my mother. Metaphor? Yes. No. If everything is metaphor, then nothing is metaphor. A man is your mother. If he is your mother, is he a man? Ask yourself rather: Is there a man who can be my mother? Is a maternal man a woman? Tell yourself rather: He is big enough and plural enough to be capable of maternal goodness.

There are daughters who are nothing but "daughters," childhood, pleasure and misfortune of childhood and dependence. And there are mothers who are not maternal, who are jealous sisters like the three or four mother–sisters of Cinderella.

And woman? Woman, for me, is she who kills no one in herself, she who gives (herself) her own lives: woman is always in a certain way "mother" for herself and for the other.

There is something of the mother in every woman. Unhappy the "woman" who has let herself be shut up in the role of a single degree of kinship! Unhappy she whom old History constrains to let herself be recruited into unjust wars, the ones that anguish and lack of love foment endlessly between mothers, daughters, daughters-in-law, sisters. These wars come from men and are profitable to them. Unhappy the daughter who learns from her "mother" to hate the mother!

In woman, mother and daughter rediscover each other, preserve each other, childhood enters into maturity, experience, innocence, the daughter in the woman is the mother-child who never stops growing.

There is something of the mother in you if you love yourself. If you love. If you love, you love yourself as well. This is the woman who belongs to love: the woman who loves all the women inside her. (Not the "beautiful" woman Uncle Freud speaks of, the beauty in the mirror, the beauty who loves herself so much that no one can ever love her enough, not the queen of beauty.) She doesn't watch herself, she doesn't measure herself, she doesn't examine herself, not the image, not the copy. The vibrant flesh, the enchanted womb, the woman pregnant with all the love. Not seduction, not absence, not the abyss adorned with veils. Plenitude, she who doesn't watch herself, doesn't reappropriate all her images reflected in people's faces, is not the devourer of eyes. She who looks with the look that recognizes, that studies, respects, doesn't take, doesn't claw, but attentively, with gentle relentlessness, contemplates and reads, caresses, bathes, makes the other gleam. Brings back to light the life that's been buried, fugitive, made too prudent. Illuminates it and sings it its names.

What moves me to write—is analogous to what moves the mother to write the universe so that the child will grasp it and name it. First I marry, I am married: I don't bar, I don't close up my lands, my senses, the carnal space that spreads out behind my eyes: I let myself be traversed, impregnated, affected (as much as possible: up to the point where, a little further and I would be lost to myself), infiltrated, invaded, medium my flesh and the immense machine of visions, of signs, that produces in a place I situate vaguely between my head and my lungs. I don't "begin" by "writing": I don't write. Life becomes text starting out from my body. I am already text. History, love, violence, time, work, desire inscribe it in my body, I go where the "fundamental language" is spoken, the body language into which all the tongues of things, acts, and beings translate themselves, in my own breast, the whole of reality worked upon in my flesh, intercepted by my nerves, by my senses, by the labor of all my cells, projected, analyzed, recomposed into a book. Vision: my breast as the Tabernacle. Open. My lungs like the scrolls of the Torah. But a Torah without end whose scrolls are imprinted and unfurled throughout time and, on the same History, all the histories, events, ephemeral changes, and transformations are written, I enter into myself with my eyes closed, and you can read it. This reading is performed here, by the being-who-wants-to-be-born, by an urge, something that wants at all costs to come out, to be exhaled, a music in my throat that wants to resound, a need of the flesh then, that seizes my trachea, a force that contracts the muscles of my womb and stretches my diaphragm as if I were going to give birth through my throat, or come. And it's the same thing.

It is impossible to say in advance what this being of air and flesh in me that has made itself out of thousands of elements of meanings taken from various domains of the real and linked together by my emotions, my rage, my joy, my desire, will be, or what it will resemble; just as there's no foreseeing the forms that lava will take as it cools. It takes on the form, the literal face, that suits the part of it that wants to be expressed. If the feeling it wants to convey is war, political battles, it flows out in theatrical form. If it's a feeling of mourning, oh! you have abandoned me, its body is sobbing, stifled breath, blanks and crises of the *Inside*.[26] If it wants to explode into orgasm, spill forth, recover, plunge, it becomes entirely *Breaths* (*Souffles*).[27]

What slowly develops in me finds its surging inscription in a form I cannot control.

So for each text, another body. But in each the same vibration: the something in me that marks all my books is a reminder that my flesh signs the book, it is *rhythm*. Medium my body, rhythmic my writing.

Two forces work on me at the same time, I am under the cosmic tent, under the canvas of my body and I gaze out, I am the bosom of happenings. And while I gaze, I listen. What happens takes place simultaneously in song. In a certain way, an opera inhabits me. What flows from my hand onto the paper is what I see-hear, my eyes listen, my flesh scans. I am invaded. I am pushed to the limit. A music floods through me, inculcates me with its staves. I am childhood, my mother sings, her alto voice. More! Encore! a lovely tongue licks at my heart, my flesh takes in the German that I can't make out. O *Lied! Leid!* Song and sorrow, blood and song! *Leid! Leib!* Sorrow and body. *Leib! Leich! Leis!* Lay, hymn, milk. *Lieb!* Love. I am loved. Letters love me. *Leise*. Soft and low. I sense that I am loved by writing. How could I help loving it? I am woman, I make love, love makes me, a *Third Body* (*Troisième Corps*)[28] comes to us, a third sense of sight, and our other ears— between our two bodies our third body surges forth, and flies up to see the summit of things, and at the summit rises and soars toward the highest things; dives, swims in our waters, descends, explores the depths of the bodies, discovers and consecrates every organ, comes to know the minute and the invisible—but in order for the third body to be written, the exterior must enter and the interior must open out. If you plug my ears, if you close my body to the outer-inner music, if you bar the song, then everything falls silent, love loses its breath, darkens, I can no longer hear myself pleasuring, I am broken, lost. What falls on the paper is what has entered my whole text through my ears.

First of all, the song of the mother the lay of the soul, I will never grow tired of them, enter, my love, feed me, my souls thirst for your voices, now I am overflowing, now the outpouring, I flow out of myself in rivers without banks; then, later on, you emerge from your own sea, you reach a shore. You make the break. Then, if you want to write books, you equip yourself, you trim, you filter, you go back over yourself, severe test, you tread on your own flesh, you no longer fly, you no longer flow, you survey, you garden, you dig, ah, you clean and assemble, this is the hour of man. You wind things up, you pull the strings, you tighten the thread, you execute the dreamwork in a state of vigilance, you cheat, condense, compile, you distill. And now what will you name it?

You dream: "The table is round. I speak louder and louder to drown out the noise, I piss harder and harder, I speak louder and louder, it takes on the force of a waterfall, hide it, I speak more and more firmly, a hydrant gushing great streams, this discourse is philosophical, hide it, what excess, all eyes on me, a pissertation, what will the outcome be?" Dreamed.

Who dreams you? Where do these messengers come from who confide in you, though in tongues that are foreign to you, the secrets of human movements, the news of peoples you've never imagined? Causing famished tribes to perish in your body, giving you infants to love who are born of your flesh but who are not your own, welcoming under your skin the thousands of anonymous enemies who harbor grudges against your life, your liberty, your sex? And from dream to dream you wake up more and more conscious, more and more woman. The more you let yourself dream, the more you let yourself be worked through, the more you let yourself be disturbed, pursued, threatened, loved, the more you write, the more you escape the censor, the more the woman in you is affirmed, discovered, and invented. And they come to you in greater and greater numbers, more exposed, naked, strong, and new. Because there is room for them in you. The more they are loved, the more they grow and expand, come close and reveal themselves as never before, the more they sow and reap femininity.

They lead you into their gardens, they invite you into their forests, they make you explore their regions, they inaugurate their continents. Close your eyes and love them: you are at home in their lands, they visit you and you visit them, their sexes lavish their secrets on you. What you didn't know they teach you, and you teach them what you learn from them. If you love them, each woman adds herself to you, and you become morewoman.

Your feminine singular unconscious: an unconscious, like that of all human beings, constituted transculturally. Cut out of History, observed by your witnesses, your magic book by more than one author, reality writes a part of it, strikes out, sorts out, cheats on another, national and transnational, millennial and instantaneous, a nutshell, a sex-sewn continent, your hundred origins program the dream-flesh. And this flesh that's been superhistoricized, museumized, reorganized, overworked, is feminine flesh; in it the "woman" projected by the Law, wounded by the same strokes of the censor that tailor an imaginary cut from a pattern—more or less skintight, clinging, incarcerating —for every woman; this little culture-sized "woman" encounters the singular life-sized woman, similar to the general woman. Like her in the movement of her instinctual economy, virtually, superabundance and dispersion, but different as one text is from another.

Write, dream, enjoy, be dreamed, enjoyed, written.

And all women feel, in the dark or the light, what no man can experience in their place, the incisions, the births, the explosions in libido, the ruptures, the losses, the pleasures in our rhythms. My unconscious is in touch with your unconscious.

Ask yourself:

How do you make meaning circulate when what comes forth is the signifier, the scene, the unfurling of hallucinating carnal sounds? Who surges up in your throat, through your muscles?

How what affects me comes into language, comes out fully worded, I don't know. I "feel" it, but it is mystery itself, which language is unlikely to let through.

All that I can say is that this "coming" to language is a fusion, a flowing into fusion; if there is "intervention" on my part, it's in a sort of "position," of activity—passive, as if I were inciting myself: "Let yourself go, let the writing flow, let yourself steep; bathe, relax, become the river, let

everything go, open up, unwind, open the floodgates, let
yourself roll . . ." A practice of the greatest passivity. At
once a vocation and a technique. This mode of passivity is
our way—really an active way—of getting to know things
by letting ourselves be known by them. You don't seek to
master. To demonstrate, explain, grasp. And then to lock
away in a strongbox. To pocket a part of the riches of the
world. But rather to transmit: to make things loved by
making them known. You, in your turn, want to affect,
you want to wake the dead, you want to remind people
that they once wept for love, and trembled with desires,
and that they were then very close to the life that they claim
they've been seeking while constantly moving further away
ever since.

Continuity, abundance, drift—are these specifically feminine? I think so. And when a similar wave of writing surges
forth from the body of a man, it's because in him femininity
is not forbidden. Because he doesn't fantasize his sexuality
around a faucet. He isn't afraid of wanting for water, he
doesn't arm himself with his Mosaic rod to smite the rock.
He says, "I'm thirsty," and writing springs forth.

Sinking into your own night, being in touch with what
comes out of my body as with the sea, accepting the anguish
of submersion. Being of a body with the river all the way
to the rapids rather than with the boat, exposing yourself
to this danger—this is a feminine pleasure. Sea you return
to the sea, and rhythm to rhythm. And the builder: from
dust to dust through his erected monuments.

The femininity of a text can hardly let itself be reined in
or corralled. Who will bridle the divagation? Who will put
the outside behind walls?

As if I were living in direct contact with writing, without

interruption or relay. In me the song which, from the moment it's uttered, gains instant access to language: a flux immediately text. No break, soundsense, singsound, bloodsong, everything's always already written, all the meanings are cast. Later if I emerge from my waters dripping all over with pleasures, if I go back the length of my banks, if from my shore I observe the revels of my dreamfish, I notice the innumerable figures they create in their dance; isn't the current of our women's waters sufficient to unleash the uncalculated writing of our wild and populous texts? Ourselves in writing like fish in the water, like meanings in our tongues, and the transformation in our unconscious lives.

# 2

## Clarice Lispector: The Approach

### Letting Oneself (be) Read (by) Clarice Lispector
### *The Passion According to C.L.*

*Clarice Lispector:* This woman, our contemporary, Brazilian (born in the Ukraine, of Jewish origin), gives us not
books but living saved from books, from narratives, re-
pressive constructions. And through her writing-window
we enter the awesome beauty of learning to read: going, by
way of the body, to the other side of the self. Loving the
true of the living, what seems *ungrateful* to narcissus eyes,
the nonprestigious, the nonimmediate, loving the origin,
interesting oneself personally with the impersonal, with the
animal, with the thing.

How to "read" Clarice Lispector: In the passion according to her: according to C.L.: writing-a-woman. What will
we call "reading," when a text overflows all books and
comes to meet us, giving itself to be lived? *Was heisst lesen?*
(What is called reading?)

At the beginning of *The Passion* Clarice cautions us, holds
us back if we are on the brink of going ahead, puts us on
(her) guard, in these worrying-reassuring terms:

*Apossiveis Leitores:*

*Este livro é como um livro qualquer. Mas eu ficaria contente se fosse lido apenas por pessoas de alma já formada. Aquelas que sabem que a aproximaçao, do que quer que seja, se faz gradualmente e penosamente— atravessando inclusive o oposto daquilo de que se vai aproximar. Aquelas pessoas que, só elas, entenderão bem devagar que este livro nada tira de ninguém. A mim, por exemplo, o personagem G.H. foi dando pouco a pouco uma alegria difícil; mas chama-se alegria.*

C.L.

*To Potential Readers:*

This book is like an ordinary book. But I would be content if it were read only by persons whose soul is already formed. Those who know that approximation, to anything whatsoever, is done gradually and painfully—and that it has to traverse even the very opposite of what is being approached. Those persons, and they alone, will understand very slowly that this book doesn't take anything away from anyone. As for me, for instance, the character G.H. has been giving me, little by little, a difficult joy, but it *is* called joy.[1]

C.L.

Toward a Least, says Hölderlin, a great beginning can come. In this Least, Clarice has us come, in order to begin.

I let myself be read according to C.L., her passion read me; and in the burning and humid current of reading, I saw how familiar and strange texts, by Rilke or by Heidegger or Derrida, had been read-already, carried away, answered, in the writing-living of C.L.

What follows is a moment of a reading of C.L.: carried out in the C.L. correspondence with all women.

I am here with C.L. now, holding steady in the room of *The Passion,* and already here, now and holding steady, in the agitation of her *Stream of Life.*[2]

## Claricewege[3]

At the school of Clarice Lispector, we learn the approach. We take lessons of things. The lessons of calling, letting ourselves be called. The lessons of letting come, receiving. The two great lessons of living: *slowness and ugliness.*

The Clarice-voice gives us the ways. A fear takes hold of us. Calls us: "There are nothing but ways." Gives-takes our hand. A deeply moved, clairvoyant fear—we take it. Leads us. We *make* ways.

Gives us the infinite: present life. Very long life because each instant *is.* Now. Each now is: a world, a life. The whole of life, including its ends, its exhaustions, its hungers, its thirsts. Leads us to love—to knowing, seeing, hearing—with our childhoods, behind the codes, the bars, the habits, to calling, behind the names, to living, behind thoughts.

Makes us hear things calling. The call there is in things: she gathers it back. The clarice voice gathers. And offers us the orange. Gives us back the thing. Precisely what the orange says to the call of her voice, its moon juice, gives it to us to drink.

The *Obst*-Voice gives us reading: the words in this voice are fruits.

Clarice reads: *Obst-Lese:* lispectorange reading.

Clarice looks: and the world comes into presence. Born things are reborn. Gathered back. For in a certain way Lispector is synonymous with *legere,* in other words "reading," in other words "gathering." Heidegger would say: "We normally understand by reading only this, that we grasp and follow a script and written matter. But that is done by gathering the letters. Without this gathering, without a gleaning [*die Lese*] in the sense in which wheat or grapes are gleaned, we should not be able to read [*Lesen*] a single word, however keenly we observe the written signs."[4]

The phrases in her voice are gardens in which I grow.

Are forests. Panthers pass by. Her phrases of soft panther
steps. Her voice, peopled, wild, listens. *Gives us the lesson
of slowness.* Slowness: the slow time that we need to approach, to let everything approach, life, death, time, the
thing; all the slowness of time that life must take in order
to give itself without hurting us too much, all the time we
must put in to reach the thing, the other, to attain it without
hurrying it, to come close to it.

Her approach is political, Clarice('s) approach: it is the
living space, the betweenus, that we must take care to keep.
Having the humility, the generosity, not to jump over it,
not to avoid it. Hurrying annuls. We are living in the time
of the flat thought-screen, of newspaper-thinking, which
does not leave time to think the littlest thing according to
its living mode. We must save the approach that opens and
leaves space for *the other.* But we live mass-mediatized,
pressed, hard-pressed, blackmailed. Acceleration is one of
the tricks of intimidation. We rush, throw ourselves upon,
seize. And we no longer know how to receive.

Receiving is a science. Knowing how to receive is the
best of gifts. Clarice gives us the example: it is a matter of
receiving the lesson of things. If we know how to think, in
the direction of the thing, letting ourselves be called to it,
the thing leads us to a space composed of the thing and of
us; of the thing and of all things. Clarice's lesson is: by
letting the thing recall something to us, we no longer forget, we un-forget, we recall the boundless other, called life.
Clarice teaches us to give ourselves, again, the time not to
forget, not to kill.

Knowing how to "see," before sight, knowing how to
hear, before comprehension, to keep the space of waiting
open. And in her language, waiting calls itself *esperar.*

What is open is time: not to absorb the thing, the other, but to let the thing present itself. Letting it produce its twenty-four faces.

Calling it quietly, praying it to come, holding out a hand to it, the word, *palavra, das Wort: "Das Wort lässt das Ding als Ding anwesen. Dieses Lassen heisse die Bedingnis."* ("The word lets the thing come into being as thing. This letting is called the thingness.")[5]

Clarice lets:[6]

In order for Spring to arrive, we have to know how to welcome it: yesterday it was already May, and it seemed to me that I no longer knew how a living day is made. It is enough to open Clarice. To look through her: and an orange tree that previously no longer was, is. In her Clarice way of opening herself up, things do not take any asking. A Spring takes hold. Clarice makes present. Gives and gives. Gives onto. Gives surely. And there is. And makes place. What we have lost. What we have never had. What we no longer knew how to have. Whose existence we were unaware of. Comes.

Every look of Clarice's: invisible gentle labor, towpath of love.

*Clarice be-dingt das Ding zu Ding.* (Clarice be-things the thing into the thing.)

Everything one must know to make possible the unveiling of a woman, to make necessary the thought of allowing the unveiling of a you—Clarice makes it come forth, makes us feel it, know it. In order for a woman to come to her, in her; because she wants her; in order for a woman to go of her own accord, and for everything to go of its own accord to our encounter. Clarice is the window. May-the-window be good:

And at once the orange enters like a bird through my breast's window.

Everything we must know how to let ourselves know of our own accord for things to arrive in their place, in their time, without our having hurried them in our blind impatience, summoned them to appear at the risk of tormenting them, of deporting them, of breaking their shell—at Clarice's school we learn to think about this. "My mystery consists of my being simply a means, and not an end, and this has given me the most dangerous of freedoms."[7]

We must learn from things; we have everything to learn from them. How to let things make themselves known by themselves, before any translation, in the Clarice way, her way of being an open window, of being a hand full of soul, of being in front of each of the innumerable lives, of coming ahead softly wide-open to meet each thing, she gives us the calling example of this.

*How to bring forth claricely:* going, approaching, brushing, dwelling, touching; allowing-entrance, -presence, -giving, -taking. Restoring things to things, giving ourselves each thing for the first time, restoring the first time of things to ourselves, each time, restoring the lost first times to ourselves.

*Das Wort, das Gebende* (The word, the giving):[8]

Clarice's calls set out, out to find the thing that remains almost without being in the windowless space, that wanders almost without a face in the space without a look, giving it all the names that make it quiver outside the space without presence, making it come back to itself, it gathers itself into itself, petals itself, fills itself out around its own heart, blushes, hastily produces a first face. And comes to be rose.

Names are hands she lays on space, with a tenderness so

intense that at last smiles a face, o, you; and the approach of her lips, and at the vase she drinks smiling.

Touching the heart of roses: this is the woman's-way of working: touching the living heart of things, being touched, going to live in the very close, going forth by tender attentive slownesses as far as the region of touch, slowly letting oneself be carried away, by the force of attraction of a rose, attracted into the heart of the rose region, staying a long time in the space of fragrance, learning to let things give us what they are when they are most alive.

We have forgotten that the world is there prior to us. We have forgotten how things have preceded us, how mountains grew up before our gaze existed, we forget how plants are called before we think to call them and recognize them, we have forgotten that it is plants that call us, when we think about calling them, that come to meet our bodies in blossom.

In these violent and lazy times, in which we do not live what we live, we are read, we are forcibly lived, far from our essential lives, we lose the gift, we no longer hear what things still want to tell us, we translate, we translate, everything is translation and reduction, there is almost nothing left of the sea but a word without water: for we have also translated the words, we have emptied them of their speech, dried, reduced, and embalmed them, and they can no longer recall to us the way they used to rise up from the things as the burst of their essential laughter, when, out of joy, they called each other, they rejoiced in their fragrance-name; and "sea," "sea" smelled of seaweed, sounded salt, and we tasted the infinite loved one, we licked the stranger, the salt of her word on our lips.

But a Clarice voice has only to say, "The sea, the sea,"

for my shell to split open, the sea is calling me, sea! calling me, waters! calls me back, and I go there, wave, I recall myself to her.

*To allow a thing to enter in its strangeness,* light from the soul has to be put into each look, and the exterior light mixed with the interior light. An invisible aura forms around beings who are looked at well. Seeing before vision, seeing to see and see, before the eyes' narrative—this is not sorcery. It is the science of the other! An art in itself; and all the ways of letting all the beings with their different strangenesses enter our proximity are regions that ask to be approached, each with an appropriate patience.

There is a patience for the egg, a patience for a rose; a patience for each particular animal; there is a patience for species, all kinds of patiences, to practice, to develop; I have some patiences that are ready to ripen, others that are germinating, others that seem not to have taken root; and it seems to me that certain clarices have worked their earth of beings so deeply that all the patiences have bloomed there. Patiences are birth-givers.

A patience pays attention. An attention that is terse, active, discreet, warm, almost imperceptible, imponderable like a light rekindling of looks, regular, twenty-one days and twenty-one nights, at the kitchen window, and at last an egg is. They pay attention: doing nothing, not upsetting, filling, replacing, taking up the space. Leaving the space alone. Thinking delicately of. Directing the mixture of knowing looks and loving light toward. A face. Surrounding it with a discreet, confident, attentive questioning, attuning to, watching over it, for a long time, until penetrating into the essence.

And sometimes we have only one patience—and then

nothing anymore; we forget, we do not give the world life, we begin and do not finish, and the world without flowers, without animals, without geology, without things, is bored to death.

We need everything. All things: all the time. Everything that has happened, everything that can happen. We need the time of presences, to approach things until they are close to us, us with them, before them, giving each to each other.

*When we set ourselves thinking, time takes shape.* We never have the time, we worry. But there is time; underneath, in immeasurable quantity, in proportion to our demands: it is enough to think and think and think, and we reach the source. Thinking gives time. And all beings, even the littlest things, are full of time: it is just up to us to think of it.

Clarice thinks: and first of all there is the kitchen. And there is an apple there. And Clarice calls the apple with such intelligence as to everything the apple signifies, contains for us, that there is at the same time in the apple the promised sustenance. And we verify the apple with our whole being. And so there is *this* apple.

All things still without a name, she attracts them, the flower, the fruit, all the anonymous, whole, not-yet-called things, each thing in its time, she makes them be there, before us, and we verify, in the same instant, how they exist how they became there, and how henceforth they are still there.

In the kitchen; and throughout the entire text hands and landscape, and in the landscape of the palm; in the text with window-sentences: each sentence opens onto another wonder.

Each sentence: ephemeral window, gaze: poem found, set down before us.

## The Putting into Work of the Egg of Art

All things that come from extremely far away, and those that come to us from the other distance, that of the very-very-near, she recalls them from the two distances.

She saves the egg from the very-very-near. She brings it back from too near.

In general, we go for years without seeing an egg come in. This is why Clarice brings us first to the school of the nearest, in the kitchen:

To get us to discover the splendor of an egg in all of its strangeness takes a much greater force than getting us to admire a mountain: in the first lesson of the egg, we learn how to bring to a chicken's egg the attention that a mountain would inspire us with. The approach to the egg is camouflaged by a veritable chain of calcareous habituations.

There was the day of the egg. The simple celebration. To say the egg is almost a Japanese art. A voice with an athletic reserve is needed. A voice for each thing. For the egg, an acrobatic voice: to launch it, to recover it, to risk it and protect it. A voice capable of surrounding each egg with delicate sounds. For gathering the first song of things, their wordless call: for saying "egg" as I say "love"; with astonishment and love; with contemplation. Whoever knows how to contemplate an egg will know how to contemplate a smile.

She has the way of calling forth this object, at that particular moment, with that color of voice that permits the event; for it is possible to see to it that an egg looked at in a certain light is a work of art.[9]

And seeing an egg is impossible, with ordinary seeing.

"In the morning in the kitchen I [Clarice] see the egg on the table."[10]

This sentence is impossible. Clarice writes it only to take it back, in the beating of writing.

"No sooner do I see an egg than I have seen an egg for the last three thousand years."[11]

Seeing? Isn't it always already having seen? Seeing is itself the egg whose shell is going to burst. Clarice teaches us superseeing. "*I never learned to look without needing more than just to see.*"[12] I cannot write "I see" while seeing, without having gone through the long labor of passion carried out in every text, at every now, to come to Seeing: the promise of one day coming to "see" the egg, this is the Passion according to C.L. One day: there will be the egg, and "*my eyes ended up not being separate from what I saw.*"[13] So this day, there is egg. This egg-day, in the present of the instant. "Try to understand what I paint and what I'm now writing. I'm going to explain: in my painting, as in my writing, I try to see strictly within the moment when I see—and not to see through the memory of having seen in an instant now past. The instant is that. The instant is of an imminence that takes my breath away. The instant is in itself imminent. At the same time that I live it, I hurl myself into its passage to another instant."[14]

A warm night broods: and at six o'clock one morning, a clarice brings about hatchings: wakes up newly astonished. The room is full of excitements that come in and go out. Wakes up ready, full of attentive ignorances, in the depths of herself, and her soul-attention gives way beneath memory, beneath the known, behind the already, beneath thoughts, and behind the thoughts, gives directly onto the path of astonishments. "I achieve a state behind thought. I refuse to divide it into words—and what I cannot and do not want to express keeps being the most secret of my secrets. I know that I'm afraid of the moments when I don't use thought and it's a momentary state, difficult to reach that, all secret, no longer uses the words with which thoughts are formed."[15]

And from astonishment to astonishment, at once completely astonished and without any astonishment, childhood Clarice lets herself be carried away, takes us to the garden of primary time, where all the different kinds of *instants* grow. And there is the treasure of events. We have only to love, be on the lookout for love, and all the riches are entrusted to us. Attention is the key.

Clarice's attention brings about hatching. Beneath her astonishment, precipitations are calmed, time lets itself be taken, moments last, grow, and bring unhoped-for births to their appointed time. And Encounters happen: there is a room there with, inside, a cockroach. And Clarice enters, by means of the cockroach, her passion according to—the Living.

And there is a grotto there, with a night around it. And there is in the grotto such a free attention that it happens that, at Clarice's call, horses respond to her ear's attention, at a gallop, and horses come in and go out like birds through the back window. And there is, in the depths of Clarice, the magical attention: attention is magical matter. The soul is the magic of attention. And the body of the soul is made from a fine, fine ultrasensual substance, so finely sensitive that it can pick up the murmur of every hatching, the infinitesimal music of particles calling to one another to compose themselves in fragrance. There is an attention for each birth. There are attentions fragile and powerful like electronic retinas that reflect for a long time to let the promise behind the appearances of things dawn, imponderable attentions that allow things to happen or not happen, according to their own movement, before their names, before, preceding our thoughts of prey, before their images, preceding our burying visions, attentions that wait, and abandon themselves to inspiration—so that things that have always been mutely present are able to make themselves heard. There is no silence. The musics of things always resound, waiting for us to hear them faithfully, with our ears, with our skin, with our nostrils, with our breathing, especially with our breasts.

Preferably, attentions move like fish in slowness. But Clarice has certain audacious attentions that go to the encounters like gentle wild beasts. "I was alert, I was completely alert. A great sense of hope arose inside me, and a surprised resignation: in this alert hope I recognized all my prior hope, I recognized too the attentiveness that I had experienced before, the attentiveness that never leaves me and that, in the final analysis, may be the thing that is most a part of my life—that perhaps is my very life itself."[16]

And they stay trembling in the very-near trembling of the other.

So woman is: the woman-and-the-other. Living ensemble, impersonal, that cannot be summarized. Or make history. But lives. Happens.

Clarice thinks of a Sunday. And there is a Sunday there. She thinks: and there is a night; and an apple, and an apple in the night; and a hand thinks toward the apple. On the way, the clarice-thought thinks of a flower. And this thought gleans itself, and there is a chrysanthemum, such as we had never looked at before. And we have an improvised lesson about flowers: with our whole body we learn that we no longer know anything about most flowers except their names as photographed flowers.

## The Imitation of the Rose[17]

There is a way of saying "tulip" that kills every tulip (*tue toute tulipe*). There is a Clarice way of making-the-tulip, and from the stem to the eye's pupils I see how the tulip is real. And I see that I had never before *seen* jasmine.

There is a way of taking a rose that would render all roses impossible: a sudden blind way of looking at it that blights it, scorches it, deroses it.

To think that, on a certain yesterday, I had really forgotten the love of flowers. And I had become very lonely. It was then that I received a bouquet of seen-flowers. On my own I would not have received them, they would have remained blurred, almost not flowers in my field of unvision. But from having been looked at with such refined respect, having been so delicately known, lit up by Clarice, each one visibly continued to remember, took pleasure in an imperceptible reviving. And thus haloed, they came to my eyes, and came to me still all wet with looking; they rose up looked-at, more clearly visible. Knowing how to see flowers: knowing how to live them. It was a bouquet of known flowers that shone, on my table, on my books, on the sheets of paper, and suddenly I understood that I was reading by the light of flowers. I learned that, for a few hours, seen-flowers give out a luster of transparent milk.

Moreover, seen–flowers call flowers to be seen, and we feel moved to run through dictionaries, fields, greenhouses; and our friends differently incarnated come to us with out-stretched arms (for we have always known that flowers are women, we have all lived one or two flowers).

At first, it is not difficult to recall flowers. For flowers love to come. They make their way naturally to an invitation.

But the problem of flowers is the problem of maternal and indispensable women: they are there. They are so much there.

"*It is their wrongdoing*": the wrongdoing of Malte Laurids Brigge's Abelone. She is so much there that she is never there for Malte, so much presence for the other, to whom she devotes herself, that she lets herself be forgotten. "*Abelone war immer da. Das tat ihr grossen Eintrag. Abelone war da, und man nutzte sie ab wie man eben konnte . . . Aber auf einmal fragte ich mich: Warum ist Abelone da?*"[18]

Let us take a rose: from the very first second, a rose takes us. In our rashness, it seems to us as if we are taking it. Because we are the ones who bear hands. By thinking this way, we take the wrong path. It is this rose that, with an infinitely sure gesture, with a rose sign verging on carmine, has left itself in our hands.

Clarice maintains: in the room, the rose spreads itself out in presence. It roses. It enters into the trance of its own presence and with all of its strength is there, with all of its contained roses, it makes the rose, for us, it delivers itself up to its I-am-a-rose in the flux of its own vitality. If we observe it in slow motion, we see that at each second the seemingly immobile rose is in full flight at the height of its presence toward our love, and enters in full radiance.

But Heidegger would say it this way: "Usage delivers what is present to its presencing, i.e. to its lingering. Usage dispenses to what is present the portion of its while. The while apportioned in each case to what lingers rests in the jointure which joins what is present in the transition between twofold absence (arrival and departure). The jointure of the while bounds and confines what is present as such. That which lingers awhile in presence, *ta eonta*, comes to presence within bounds (*peras*)."[19]

It is not by chance that Clarice had this story with a certain rose. Among all the plants, the rose is the one whose way of sharing its presence in the movement of its blossoming is the most human: the soft giving of a rose today helps us to take the giving of all presence. By its way of containing while overflowing, of making us feel the rose of the rose, of making us think in its blossoming of the mystery of the birth of the living in each instant we do not forget to share. To receive sharing. Our loving souls are descendants of roses. The Clarice rose is giving. Does the rose give us more than a rose?

The rose that gave itself to be taken by Clarice was so well taken that at the same time it made her the present of a secret: it survived to give her proof of the strength now produced in the alliance uniting two beings around the same need to call, to respond, to take source. To give source to the source.

*Diese Rose aus Bewegung* (This rose that is made out of movement). From a bird, the sky rises. From a rose, time breaks free. The rose also gives us the movement of presence. Rilke writes twenty-four poems *on* the rose. But Clarice gives the rose's silent breathing to be *lived:* reality has no synonyms.

To get to the heart of the rose, we have only to take the rose's path, to go to it according to its way. Approaching with such an absence of self, with such lightness, without disturbing its proximity, entering with fragrant steps its fragrant water without disturbing it. Now there is a rose in the room. In the space opened by its coming, we live. And turtles?

Now, maintaining, and keeping the same elements, the same tenderness, the same respect, Clarice can replace a rose with a turtle. But Rilke could replace it only with a unicorn or an anemone. But Clarice with a cockroach. But Rilke no. But Clarice with an oyster. But Rilke only in lacework. "I see the flowers in the vase. They're wildflowers that were born without having been planted. They're yellow. But my cook said: 'What ugly flowers.' Only because it's difficult to love what's common. Behind my own thought is the truth that is the world's. The illogic of nature."[20]

For at Clarice's school we have the most beautiful of lessons: *the lesson of ugliness.* "Have I in effect abandoned a whole system of good taste? But is that my only gain? How imprisoned I must have been that I feel myself freer just because I no longer fear a lack of aesthetics . . . I still don't foresee what else I may have gained. Maybe I'll learn of it little by little. For now, the first timid pleasure that I feel is being able to say that I have lost my fear of the ugly. And that loss is a very great good. It is a delight."[21]

There is Rilke, but there is Clarice. There is only: There is fear, there is cult, there are limits, there is the reserved expanse of the *Weltinnenraum:* the world-in-the-intimacy-of-myself-Rilke. There is closure; the hand holds, writing elects through reading and contains. But there is Clarice, there is audacity, boundless vertigo, there is yes: "I want the unconcluded. I want the profound organic disorder that nevertheless triggers the intuiting of an underlying order. The great power of potentiality. These, my stammered sentences, are made the very moment they're being written and they crackle they're so new and still so green. They are the now. I want the experience of a lack of structure. Although my text is transversed from beginning to end by a fragile conductive line—what is it?"[22]

There is the Clarice-risk. Clarisk: through the horrible to Joy. For Clarice has the terrifying splendor of daring the real, which is not beautiful, which is not organized, of daring the living, which is not symbolized, which is not personal, of being in the kernel of the *is* that is without the self, of writing by the flow of signs without history.

Dares, wants, cliché without base, the poor, the lowly, the ephemeral, of each instant. Is not afraid, wants the truth, the living, which has no meaning; the infinite endurance of the living. Is afraid only of being afraid. Goes. Does not hold herself back. Loses herself. Keeps herself only from lying. "But the fact is that truth has never made sense to me. Truth doesn't make sense! That's why I was afraid of it, and still am. Forsaken as I am, I give everything over to you—so you can do something pleasant with it. If I talk to you will I frighten you and lose you? But if I don't, I'll lose myself and in losing myself lose you anyhow."[23]

*The Passion According to G.H.:* the passion of being in impersonal living adherence to the big immemorial Brazilian cockroach, our ancestor: *Barata.*

I'm achieving a higher plane of humanity. Or of inhumanity—the *it.*

What I do by involuntary instinct cannot be described.

What am I doing in writing you? I'm trying to photograph perfume . . .

I write you this facsimile of a book, the book by someone who doesn't know how to write; but in the most ethereal realms of speech I almost don't even know how to speak . . .

So when I write you I respect the syllables.

. . . Now I'm going to light a cigarette. I might go back to the typewriter, or I might stop here for good . . .

I'm back. I am thinking about turtles . . . They interest me very much. All living beings, man notwithstanding, are a riot of wonderment: we were formed and there was a lot of raw material left over—*it*—and then the animals were made. Why a turtle? Perhaps the title of what I'm writing to you should be something like this, phrased as a question: "And turtles?" You who read me would say: "It's true that it's been a long time since I thought about turtles."[24]

The imitation of the turtle. Of the cockroach. Of the chair. Of the egg. "Taking care of the world also requires a lot of patience: I have to wait for the day an ant will appear."[25] There must be a wait long enough to save the ant. A waiting that is precise enough, powerful, woman enough.

And woman?

There must be a wait so powerfully thoughtful, open, toward beings so close, so womanly-familiar that they are forgotten for it, so that the day will come in which the women who have always been—there, will at last appear.

# 3

## Tancredi Continues

I read *Jerusalem Delivered* headlong, throwing myself into lost bodies, troubled bodies, delimited bodies.

Two camps dispute the body of the Beloved. I mean Jerusalem. Two camps, always the same ones. Today just as at the time of the Crusades, and just as in Paradise.

But it is not the story of the war between the Faithful and the Unfaithful that interests me; it is the other story, the one hidden by history, the one of two beings, two others who cannot remain prisoners in their camps, do not want to win the war, but want to win life or lose it. What holds me is the story of love, in other words the story of the other and the other's other. Not Rinaldo and Armida, Same-Couple. But the Others, the irrepressible ones, Tancredi, Clorinda, the lovers of freedom, these two singular creatures, stronger than themselves, yes, the one and the other capable of going, at the price of life, for the love of truth, for love, beyond their own forces, all the way to the other —the farthest, the nearest. The two always-others, who dare to achieve Departure. Even madder, and wiser, then Torquato Tasso, who created them much freer than himself in a dream. Stranger. Absolutely faithful—to their own human secret—to their own being more-than-man more-than-woman. With courage they do not know themselves, with nobility they do not possess themselves, with humility they do not restrain themselves, do not withhold themselves, both agree to surrender themselves, to the point of approaching the other. I no longer know whether my "they" is masculine or feminine.

What grips me is the *movement* of love. The violently described curve from one soul to the other body, from one sexed body to another gender of body, from a smile to a gaze. *Gracious* exchange (yes: it is a question of beautiful *coups de grâce*) from one pleasure to the other whose sex is not revealed. It is a question of the grace of genders instead of the law of genders, it is a question of dancing, of the aerial crossing of continents. It is a question in front of Jerusalem, *still only obscurely,* of the mystery of love, which is a question of acrobatics: fly or fall! There is no turning back, it is straight ahead. That is why it is so easy. Yes or No—there is no in-between. That is why loving is never difficult except in appearance. Because the opposite of "easy" is not "difficult": it is only *impossible.* So is love the secret of acrobatics? It is trust, yes: the desire to cross over into the other. The acrobat's body is his soul.

Is the crossing vertiginous? Like every crossing. Useless to contemplate or fathom what separates: the abyss is always invented by our fear. We leap and there is grace. Acrobats know: do not look at the separation. Have eyes, have bodies, only for there, for the other.

Tancredi-is-for-Clorinda-is-for-Tancredi.

If Tancredi is "lost for love" for Clorinda, it is for Tancredi that he is lost, but for Clorinda he is more than gained: given.

I wonder: Why can only Tancredi love Clorinda? Go as far as her? Leave the self to orient himself toward the other?

I follow Tancredi and Clorinda through forests, battlefields, the war between races, religions, over enclosures, chasms, beyond ramparts, literary genres and genders and others, as far as the wild songs of Rossini.

Then I listen to Tancredi soaring toward his inner Jerusalem on the wings of the hippogriff Music, and returning to us melodiously, strangely, other . . .

For in the interval, between the unconsciouses, between the stanzas and measures, between Tasso and Rossini, the story has shifted a little:

In the place of the sumptuous Clorinda, the most ardent, adorable, and vulnerable of knights, there suddenly appears a woman of equal force, but with no other armor than her soul. From the armor-clad Clorinda, Amenaide emerges utterly disarmed, impregnable in that she is so little threatening, still more powerfully woman, more strongly Clorinda.

And Tancredi? I don't know . . . I hear his voice, its sweetness, its fury, I hear the high mezzo voice of the Enigma. The Enigma? Yes: the answer: only Tancredi can love Amenaide, who lives in the heart of Clorinda. Only s(he).

Only (s)he? Yes. This Tancredi can really only be a Tancreda; this is what Rossini feels and I also feel it, but I don't know how to speak of it. Because it is the Enigma: it doesn't explain itself, it makes itself heard.

Listen.

I say Tancreda, I'm not saying a woman; I could, but nothing is that simple.

Listen: Rossini doesn't say that the hero, in order to be Tancredi, must be haunted by a woman's voice. He performs it.

There is no explanation. There is simply singing. He

makes it a condition of the body that for a man to love a woman the way Tancredi loves Clorinda or Amenaide, he must be a woman—I mean, Tancredi.

If it is enigmatic, so much the better. Because if it were not, we would no longer have the least bit of life work to do.

We have to go around the world, around Jerusalem, lose memory, lose knowledge, in order to arrive at the depths of real love, where we never know when we love, who we love, in whom we love. Tancredi loves Clorinda. Does Tancredi not know who in Clorinda is loved by whom in him? A moment ago it was a man; a second ago a woman; but was it really that?

One more remark before I lose myself: Clorinda "knows" that she is a "woman." Rossini's Tancred(a) does not: (she) is a Tancredi, only God knows this, and perhaps Rossini a little—as for us, our musical body "knows" it, though we may be unaware of it.

Now I am completely lost. All I can offer you at this point is to (mis)lead you into the space where Tancredi lives and burns to be woman.

But I also want to meet a particular someone/no one and to love her beyond the true and false that mark the two extremes, ends, limits, of "reality."

I want to love a person freely, including all of her secrets. I want to love in this person someone she doesn't know.

I want to love outside (the) law: without judgment. Without imposed preference. Does that mean outside morality? No. Only this: without fault. Without false, without true. I want to meet her between the words, beneath language.

I wanted to look at *Tancredi:* magical voices carried me

away, whinnying, murmuring, far away from myself, far away from us, far away from the opera, to the other side.

I want to meet her intimately, behind gestures, words, activities, in the region of mysteries. Still alone, or alone once again. And above all uncertain, yes, always already a little strange, because it is only in society and appearance that a person of such depth presents a united, determined surface. But as soon as everyone is gone she hurries into her room, and even before changing or removing her makeup she abandons herself with joyous relief to her vital uncertainty, she collapses on the bed like a piece of scenery, and there she stretches herself and becomes, once again, she-knows-not-who.

I know that if I say "woman" or "man" one more time, and quite simply (as I have done, as we do, as we have all done, which is why I do it too), I won't be able to shake the words off either myself or her (and we will end up no longer loving those whom we love, and we will deceive ourselves until we no longer love). I would like at least once to try to say what I am trying to think, with difficulty, already, about this question of gender: because I feel that she (this person) probably consciously inflicted it on herself, or at least mysteriously suffered from its effects: I feel it in her way of throwing herself on the bed when she is alone, as if she were leaping out of someone else, in her way of stretching herself vigorously and roaring softly, of rolling about on her long flanks, of sleeping for a while. And it is only after a dream that she shudders, goes abruptly to the bathroom mirror. And looks at herself there, asks herself, knitting her brow, whether it shows on her face that she doesn't know. And also because in the evening she, too, listens to *Tancredi* while watching the night rising through the window.

So it is a question of the mystery of "woman" and "man." Are these words the proper names of two mysteries or of one?

I *feel* the truth of this mystery: mysterious and true. I feel its truth but I don't know how to say it truthfully.

Now, musicians have never lost the sense of the mysterious, which is the song of truth. What sings in a "man" is not him, it is her. They have always known it.

But we, who speak, we lose, we lose, I am losing now.

But what suffers and rejoices under "Orpheus" is a woman voice.

She listens to Gluck, Mozart, and Rossini because they knew, too. How to live crying out with frightened joy over the pitfall of words.

Fortunately, when someone says "woman," we still don't know what that means, even if we know what we want to mean.

And so I wonder what is man and what is woman and what am I, which is what she, in the bathroom, is wondering too, while I no longer know when I say "a woman" if I am talking about a person you would call "a woman" or if . . .

In any case, she is not *a* woman. She is plural. Like all living beings, who are sometimes invaded, sometimes populated, incarnated by others, drawing life from others, giving life. Who do not know themselves.

And so, if I were to talk about a person I had met and been overwhelmed by, while she herself was also moved, and I was moved to see her moved, and she, seeing that I was moved, was moved in turn, and if this person were a

she and a he and a s(he) and a (s)he and a shehe and a heshe,
I would want permission not to lie, I do not want to stop
her if she goes into a *trans,* I want him to, I want her to, I
will follow them.

And a person who looks like a "man" full of woman
hidden behind this look, what do you call such a person,
and a woman full of woman in whom still another lives, I
don't know, were it not for the suggestion of the look, and
the name, the facial makeup, and all of the other
makeups . . .

Time to listen to *Fidelio* again.

Even if I feel clearly that the more I try to say, the more
I have wandered astray, far from what, beneath appearances
and secretly and obscurely, I am sure I understand—I think.


I should also say that in order to know him better inter-
nally, I close my eyes, I avoid looking her straight in the
face because it is not impossible that at first sight she may
look a little like one of these men who are not at all feminine, but who are capable of this slow inner dance, who
have a loving, elastic rapport with the earth and are thus a
bit f... thus in short a bit m... and thus . . .

And then I feel her so clearly and again I know without
any doubt how lightly powerful she is like a man who is
powerful lightly like a woman who is powerfully light like
a man who is gently powerfully powerful like a woman of
powerful tenderness . . .

And all I wanted to try to say is that she is so infinite.


One does not guess anything: one knows.

Before meeting the-one-whose-name-I-still-have-not-spoken, I "knew" that she listens to *Tancredi,* in the evening, when she is alone, and watches the night falling through the window before her, royal, comes the night draped in her satins of dark blue steel, comes slowly toward her, pensive darkly brilliant, and the armor which covers her allows only her head to be seen; she is a Persian night. She sees her, is amazed by her blacks, by her clouds, by her swirls, and listening to the dark brilliance rising, behind her, from out of the depths of the room, of time, she hears the voice that reigns over her heart, the sea-mother-voice, which was already calling her thirty-five years ago, lulling her, awakening her.

The Third Song in *Jerusalem Delivered* takes two hours to listen to, and in reality a day and a night. And during all this time Tancredi and Clorinda do not meet each other, do not meet each other, time almost comes to a halt.

But seen from the top of a fig tree overlooking the wall of Salem, the song can be contained in these few words:

"The Christian army approaches Salem—Clorinda overpowers the Christians—Tancredi flies to their rescue—Bouillon prepares to attack Salem."

And between times—Clorinda brushes against Tancredi —between arrows—Tancredi flies—and between words the earth disappears, time has no time, Tancredi Clorinda, seen from outside, fly (but their flight is not rapid enough, time runs out, never, seen from above, will they meet).

But inside the song, God grants them all the time they need to slip toward one another, all of the time between possibility and impossibility, and inside there is no impossibility, love knows no "no," nor do desire, the text, the unconscious, know what time it is. God gives them the grace to slip in between the sexes alive . . .

When they slipped into this opening, its silence vibrating, in harmony, with the sweet, muted sound of violins, then I saw them.

Tancredi haunted by Clorinda, haunted by Amenaide, haunted by Sutherland, haunted by Tancredi, haunted by Horne, haunted by Tancredi, and I, too, enchanted.

## Ourselves We Do Not Owe[1]

I did not see them come in. It was a single apparition for me, but they slipped in as if they had been coming forever or from having forever just taken shape.

I saw them slip in, one all in white, the other all in dark blues, like—not a woman—not a man—not only—like—the personification of the mystery—of humankind—like humanity in person, brooding over its own mystery, which is obviously neither man nor woman, which is two to begin with, two people, being-itself, with its mystery which is to be a question posed in the direction of the other, and only the other has the answer, has only this answer to give, to the other but not to the self, and this is how I suddenly saw them slipping down along the same musical question between them a single silence accompanied so softly, and between them a question accorded itself, answered itself, like a question that gives itself to the question that comes forth to meet it, musically grants it the ever-sought-after answer.

Because it is only the perfect harmony of two questions that will give an answer.

That is why there are so few answers in the world, there are so many questions, and so many books, so much hope, and despairing, and so many traces of error, but so few of music, of answers asking themselves, with the questions perching on their laps, eyes closed, listening, listening, there are so few. Because only two questions in perfect harmony end up composing an answer: that is, two questions moving toward each other with the same sustained rhythm, as two arrows shot forth at the same moment by two equal archers from the two sides of the mountain ascending like two alto voices soaring from the two shores of the sea above the orchestra will perhaps end up meeting above the summit, if a storm does not intervene. A storm, or history.

But first the chance of the answer is a question of body. Then of culture, history, all the rest. And in the end, the truth is perhaps that only the questions that harmonize to answer each other had begun to answer from the start, had perhaps never even turned toward each other to ask, but already, committing and giving themselves to each other, had begun to rise up in reply, up through the air alongside the slopes like a bird perched on an arrow, and on the other side this unparalleled thing had also occurred, so that when the arrows at the height of their trajectory obey the laws of physics, the two birds catch sight of each other from a distance, and free, meet each other above the clouds, where we can no longer see them but we can hear their triumphant cry very clearly.

To return to my two precious apparitions: to tell the truth, as soon as I saw them gliding toward each other, because of the suppleness of their movement, I guessed. Perhaps because of their look of astonishment, gently astonished, remaining astonished, as if to greet each other close up as well as from far away? Gliding, yes, all in whites, one shining forth to meet the other all shimmering in deep blues, and the whites, too, created a depth, a density, like two fates: as if they felt each other inevitable. Not the way a woman walks, and, graceful or awkward, she is woman-walking, and it wasn't a man who was coming closer, not simply man-approaching who came. No, before me they slipped, like two boats gliding over the water, as if each were at the mercy of the other. Drawn to each other, beholding each other with one imperceptible movement, falling lightly, with their whole body, holding each other with their eyes, holding back with a look from the brim of their eyes, wondering, asking: Why me? In the same sweet silence accompanied by twelve violins, thinking the whole time, astonished, not speaking, as if they were thinking that it was the last time they would be able to look at each other and question each other, and still not know, Who me? Why me? Who? Me who . . .

Why me? Standing, very close now, both the same height, they could have touched, there was hardly any astonishment left now, but they continued to be astonished: "Why am I in white, and the other coming night-blue to meet the day . . . ?"

"Why?" they ask each other, giving themselves as an answer, draped in many silks, and the astonishment swells their breasts, with their whole body asking each other and saying: "Because it's you," and the musical harmony of the astonishment is the answer.

(I am well aware that I am in the process of not gaining the resolve to make the evidence visible. I am afraid, I won't hide it, because I have a secret to tell which is so beautiful it dazzles me, and if I am not able to dazzle you, I will have committed a crime against everything that I venerate, life, beauty, desire. Because one must reveal the secrets, but in their splendor. Otherwise, if one repeats without dazzling, one violates the secret of the secret; it is sexuality without God. Do I have enough strength to raise the secret of this story above my head? Do I have the heroic serenity, the male femininity? These are the virtues that my respect for this vision requires.)

I follow them . . .

So high, painfully trying to give herself to Tancredi, Amenaide is no more than a look, how deeply she wants to die with her eyes open, her look never leaving his eyes, to fade out in his night like the sun, and Tancredi in the same astonishment is no more than a pair of eyes, and, for a fraction of a second, together, they nearly die, they forget the world and slip into eternity.

I see them very close up then, I see their madness, their secret:

He was the most handsome of a woman, the most majestic of women, he was radiant with woman majesty.

And more lovely than a young man, more handsome than a knight of the faith, she was noble with heroic strength.

He the most proudly erotic of wild creatures.

She the pitiless passion, unyielding bravery of love.

Just what it was. What I saw; and what they saw, too.

Why me? were struggling now as if they were about to enter each other.

And the weapons signified: I beg of you, vainquish me but do not wound me.

Slipping toward each other like night toward the day.

Tancredi falls like the night, high up, full of dreams, and

so profound and all ice on the outside, but with a burning heart, like the night which adores and does not know itself.

Falls large and delicate and male on the outside, but under the dark blue star-studded armor reigns the burning humility of a woman who loves.

And what I saw, blazing Amenaide sees it, too, even if her apparel eclipses the whiteness of the snow crowning the summit of the Alps, she is lofty only to the depth of her profound humility, if he is the woman lover, she is the man who loves . . .

This is what I wanted to say.

In a dream I saw a pure turquoise. Sobbing, I reach out and try to grasp it. It is in the middle of the sky. It is above my life, like my own external heart. I want it, I see it, I want it the way that Tancredi wants his beloved dead or alive wants her alive to the point of death, the way human beings need the secret of their own lives. I see it shining, the splendor of my existence, my external treasure, I see above my head the meaning of my whole story. A single night separates me from it. I try to cross it. I hold out my hands, I am sobbing with rage, I have it at the tips of my fingers.

The sky is near, only one transparent night away.

Inside the turquoise gleams a fascinating pearl.

My life burns to rise above itself toward my secret. I burn my soul so that a flame will reach higher, closer, than me, but what rises highest higher closer to the turquoise is smoke, and, eyes full of tears, I sob with hope.

The why of my life is a turquoise that I could hold in my right hand. I burn for a tiny double star. Because it is so infinitely pure. My secret is the star of Evidence. At the heart of it lies a soft gleaming pearl like the flash of eternity at the heart of a moment. My star that still has no name!

My secret is no bigger than a hazelnut of eternity.

Only one night still holds back my hand.

I see what my turquoise means. A dark blue silence before my lips holds back my words in a nebula.

My turquoise contains its most precious part. An opaque pearl is the secret of its transparency. The secret of the royal blue is the infinite whiteness of its depths.

I can only sob what I wanted to say.

Tancredi leaned closer, asking himself so blue slowly as if it were the last time they would look at each other from so far away how is it that you are so white looking so closely at each other, looking closer as the adored woman looks in the mirror for the secret of this adoration, asking it, who is loved, wondering, who is she, the one who is adored in me, does not look at herself, tries to discover the secret that the other cherishes, looks painfully beneath her own features for the soul of the other, as high and noble and silent Amenaide favored by the night glides along and her heart burns contemplating the why of her life which shines blue attracts her and answers her royally blue mysterious and so close, why are you so blue?

I ask myself: One day will I understand the secret of this love which I feel and which at the touch of my fingers, at the touch of my words, fades away? One day will I understand the night? Will I know who understands me?

I saw their secret. What I am telling of it is no more than light turned to dust. He was so handsome, one felt he was beautiful. And she was not only a beautiful woman, she was handsome: I am telling what one could see:

The two of them come swooping down on each other like two enemies.

Want to have the measure of each other, urged on by desire, have elected each other,

In the darkness do not meet

(At this point, an outburst of song shook the night, and I scribbled down all that I heard, breathless phrases, on bits of paper, eyes on them, hand noting blindly):

Night day both he and she
Spring forth, still don't meet
What do you want of me, what are you bringing me
Leave you I'd rather die
Why were you searching for me, me, so ardently
As if you knew me
As if I knew you
My fiancée I beg you to tell me your name
Since fate, since destiny have so ordained
I will not reveal my name, my real name
As if you knew me
Open their arms and spring forth
If it were war they would not miss each other,
But it's not war, it's love, they brush against each other
Do not embrace, it's the war of love
Let her breathe if he can
You are no longer my sister
I am no longer your child
The anger and darkness are neither feigned nor
    measured
Their feet are immobile, their souls are restless, excited,
    the swords come down, broadside, or point first,
What are you fleeing, my love? Standing together. Do
    not see each other . . .

Nothing separates them,
What separates them? The dark malice of History
The struggle forces them closer and closer,
Already they can't use the point anymore,
They blind each other with looks
Three times Amenaide receives Tancredi's look
Three times she breaks free from this attraction she
    fears
Believe you, I'd rather die
But with my whole life, in spite of myself, I believe
    you
You are no longer my child
I am no longer your sister.
Finally, exhausted, they draw back to breathe for a
    moment
Attentive and silent like two adversaries
Asking themselves, who will vanquish, love, death . . .
Then what sweetness when all pain is exhausted
When anger no longer has any blood, anguish is no
    longer sustained
Then what respect.

I do not see what could separate them. Two beings, each made for the other, apparently neither sister nor brother and nevertheless of equal measure and equally without measure.

One can see that they are attuned to each other in every way, like a royal soprano to an alto capable of the highest notes, one can see that they are a match for each other in differences and in likenesses, the one enhances and brightens the other. The two of them equal in stature, in power, in richness of soul, in mobility of spirit, equal in virtue, and different in feature, in color, in resonance, like . . . like Sutherland and Horne, for example.

One sees nothing separating them. Only an imperceptible vibration. A delay, as in life.

Will they end up lips upon lips, taking each other and breathing life into each other again? I still think so. It would be a true misfortune if it were not so.

I felt a vague fear. There was an ever so light trembling in their breathing. As if they were silently struggling together against a word, a single terrible word, with all of their forces focused inward, leaning over the wall, afraid of being surprised by an enemy who was unique but as powerful and cunning as poison, who would not come from the present, but could escape, like jealousy itself, from a very ancient and unhappy time.

But thus occupied in not letting themselves be surprised by the infernal word, they had not yet had the sweet leisure to say I love you.

They look at each other a little breathlessly, their eyes begging each other with a tenderness that would turn a lioness into a faithful ally, and they lean their exhausted bodies on their swords.

> Yet, with the impossible between them, do not leave
>     each other,
> The impossible unites them like the night
> In which they lose discover themselves each other
> *Amie!* Beloved! In your cruel destiny I will remain
>     faithful to you
> Why should this be impossible? Because it was night?
> Because it was day? Why shouldn't it be possible?
> *Amie,* in your faithful destiny I will remain cruel to
>     you.

(And yet I felt vaguely that they were still searching, either one was weighed down or the other was losing a certain lightness. I don't know who said:

> I should embrace her I can't
> I should confront her I can't
> I should flee from her

I do not want to know who could not keep from fleeing, from falling.

Was it misfortune? The truth is, there was mistrust. But that was in another story.)

So I do not know whom I started to love, suddenly, with all the weight of my own desire, in vain. I was in love with one with the other. With both of them. Because of the other I loved. One because the other. One for and against the other.

> Yes she is the object of my passion
> She, the object of my pain,
> This slow passion which threatens one toward the
>     other,
> This tormenting hope, all growing in my heart,
> This apprehension, this confidence,
> This wonder, all growing,
> This belief, this nonbelief,
> This passion which grieves my heart and enchants me,
> It is she too that I adore, I don't know why,
> Love surprised me as I was watching
> Two great ones look at each other for the last time,
> Caught hold of me in her big, strong but delicate arms
> And I fell, astonished,
> In love,

Not just with the one I wanted to love,
The one I loved in advance, because she was blue and
    dark
And ardent and profound like someone I had loved
    before
But, astonished, I fell also into the musical aura
Of the one I was not thinking of, the other, white and
    gold,
The pure spontaneous and confident one, she too,
At the last moment, and because one was the answer
    that the other didn't dare hope for and with all her
    soul humbly hoped for.

Each amplifies the other, each is magnified by the other. Each all the greater and more magnificent for mysteriously understanding the other.

Is Tancredi a woman ending, or a man beginning to be a woman in order to be a man?

But my God, I am only me, I am only a woman, how can I express what is more than me? I divine what is more than a woman, what is more than a man, but above me everything sparkles and dazzles me and merges into a single person with athletic aspirations, rather tall for a woman, yes, she seems to me to be a woman but set naturally in the bearing of a man, like my pearl in turquoise.

What do you call a person who looks rather more like a woman with dark blue eyes, an icy look in appearance, burning inside, who is large and imposing like the night, and stars nuzzle up against her full breast, closing their eyes in love, who fights like a hero, would give up her life like a mother, and who sheds tears of impatience and grief, and who dreams of destiny only as love, and who takes fortresses more easily than a kiss, and her voice is so deep and warm and moist, it sounds like the sea of human tears, and every woman not bound by the cords of marriage who hears it, feels the burning need to immerse herself in it?

In this story she bore the name of Tancredi, his past, his arms. Help, Mozart, Rossini, help, number without gender, gender without limit!

When does woman begin when does one become other when continues when pursues when finally touches finally embraces?

No; I should rather ask:

Where does man begin woman begin continue?

Continues

Yet—already the last stars were paling with the first fires of dawn and yet the struggle continued forward.

Tancreda was worrying about the fatal triumph.

Continuing in an alto voice into which I wanted to pour all my tears:

> Must I yield? Must I vanquish? Who?
> Who are you, please, victor or vanquished, tell me, so I
>     will know whom I save, whom I lose.
> Speak to me: I'm not listening: Speak to me.
> You alone have been loved by my heart.
> How can I help believing you.
> Only I must believe the impossible,
> So *Adieu*.
> What do you want? To leave you. To follow you.
> Two fighters. Two adversaries side by side against the
>     impossible
> Yes, you are the object of my pain
> They do not strike. Contemplate each other.
> Turn away from each other. Flee from each other.
> As if they were falling upon each other.

(There are several Tancredis, which is why I have so much trouble trying not to mislead us. I promise that I will do the impossible to explain myself on this subject as soon as broad daylight arrives.)

I feel clearly that I am on the inside of the night and yet before my own night. I feel that I am before the mystery that I am destined to encounter and not resolve. Tancreda, Amenaide, these first two are the figures of my mystery. Everything that I write, it seems to me, leads me myopically to their embraces, and then I feel that everything is happening right there before my hopelessly wonderstruck eyes, the meaning of the mystery catches fire, a cry explodes in my breast—as if I were "discovering" the "truth" of "love" (all these words are smoke choking the pure point of my cry)—and—*fiat nox!*

But perhaps what is most difficult and most necessary is really to forget the judges who make us stupidly answer their stupid summons, make us justify the nonjustifiable, speak of silence, crush music under the millstone of words, lie by swearing to tell only their truth, plead guilty to a lack of absence and a lack of weakness, make excuses for every thought; really to forget, which means forgetting fearlessly, quickening the pace with a bound, without ever forgetting them in reality, flinging a glistening forgetfulness over our shoulders and making headlong for the free-soul zone into which they cannot venture because they perish on contact with pure air.

After our oppressive and inflexible era, I would like to live in a time in which the tongue would not be bound, castrated, intimidated, constrained to obey fraudulent sages and genuine asses.

But sometimes I am stopped by the word-police,

searched, interrogated and counter-interrogated. Sometimes I am the one who stops; thinking, perhaps mistak-
enly, that I must show all the same that I am not afraid of
the insults being hurled at us. I turn around, I respond, and
the struggle begins, to the cries of Women! Women! hurled
out, picked up in hatred, in love. In the din of the argu-
ments, one no longer knows what one is attacking, what
one is defending, the words change in meaning depending
on the speakers, now blessings, now curses.

I am well aware that the best way to defend a given truth
is never to pronounce its name, never to expose it to public
abuse. From so much usage, the word "Jewish" is getting
dry as a fossil. And this is the case with the word "Polish"
at this particular moment. Yet it is a necessity of our time.
At this particular moment, not saying the word "Polish" is
like denying a child of one's own. (This is also the case of
the word "true," accused, in our aged time, of being too
good to be true.)

And at this time there are so many clandestine massacres
of women that a woman has to say "woman" a dozen times
a day in order to protest.

But by constantly saying "I am a woman," we end up
creating various forced truths. And worst of all, the more
we say it in order not to be swept far from our own banks
by the current, and the more securely we moor ourselves
to avoid being swept away from one another, the more we
contribute to reinforcing limitations of strength, to restrict-
ing native territories and fortifying prejudices. We are
closed in, we enclose ourselves, we enwoman ourselves.
And worst of all, what had been the sweet and inexplicable
and intimate truth, the magic hand on the heart, beneath
which we could faint with joy, becomes a sentence.

So the truth, which appears inside of the night, in the

warm depths of a dream, and then only, peacefully un-
dresses before me and smiling comes slipping I do not know
how over my innermost body, and caresses my heart, and
—then—the sweet softness of her breasts—and this is what
absolute knowledge is—(it isn't surprising if what I am
writing is not sufficiently clear, since not a single word ever
returns from the luminous depths where our truth lives.
The few words that come close are transformed into
sighs)—so the truth which only lives in the shelter of silence
is forced to appear, and then is like a fish pulled from the
water, thinking in a final convulsion of the sea, then, the
end.

But in this night full of voices, I am bewildered between
two Tancredis. Is the one the other or the same or the
hidden truth or the manifest truth of the other? Here I am,
between one and the other, astonished, stubbornly refusing
to take my eyes off the mystery: as if I wanted to become
conscious of my unconscious as I immerse myself in it.
Here I am, under the sea with my lantern. I circle around
inside a question, like a Chinese fish in a swimming pool. I
am here and I am all at sea: I imagine there is an answer
outside.

"Why is it necessary for this Tancredi to be a Tancreda?"

But there is no outside. My swimming pool is infinite. It
is the world.

Let's not think. Let's swim.

There are two Tancredis. They are not altogether the
same, are almost the same. Tancredi of Jerusalem, is he
Tancredi of Syracuse or is she not?

It is because he insisted on knowing what he was thinking

that Tancredi turned against himself in an ultimate furious effort to come to grips with himself.

These are things to dream of.

I am swimming between two Tancredis, the water is almost a night starred with serenity. I am dreaming along in the very substance of eroticism, as if music had finally once more become what it was, musical wave. I am swimming between little waves of thoughts:

The enigma is cool inside, I feel good here, love glides along in pursuit of itself, from Jerusalem to Syracuse and back again, the appearance changes and reality blushes with emotion.

First of all, it is the story of a Tancredi, who loves a hero who is a woman who in reality is a hero who is a woman, and if he loves her it is because she is a woman. And so is he.

And there is a Clorinda, who is a woman with the strength to take on a man's appearance and who is all the more one because the other. In the end, I am not sure. And so Tancredi is the person who loves this woman.

So Rossini guesses: for a man to love as Tancredi loves this woman who is this still and more, he had to be a woman.

I am lost . . .

So much the better . . . Tancredi can only be a woman when he is a man. Or no? Tancredi can only be a woman when she is a man?

A-man-who-loves-a-woman-as-if-he-were-a-woman has a voice that traverses life, death, walls, sands, superstitions, magnificent armor, shields, images, languages, meanings; neither race nor color, nor one gender nor another gender, hold it captive, it is made to celebrate she

who inspires it. Tancredi sings a woman: a woman sings
Tancredi . . .

Tancredi, a woman . . .

If I love a woman, I will call her Tancredi.


Astonished Tancredi astonished Tancreda understands
Clorinda, and for Rossini, it is obvious, "Tancredi" is a
woman in a man.

But for the Christians and for all of Jerusalem, it is
Clorinda who is a woman in a man.

And there I see them hurl themselves toward each other
faster than the movement of my gaze, they swoop down,
their steeds raising a cloud of shining dust, I can no longer
see them, I can only hear the voices measuring each other,
the lioness pouncing, the eagle rending the air; I can hear
two voices, one is a woman's and the other one is a woman's too, rushing headlong toward each other, one of them
is not a woman, one of them is not only a woman, the one
is not simply the opposite of the other.

> What a secret!
> O heaven you know for whom I tremble
> Because he doesn't know who she is
> Doesn't know he is a woman
> Because with what difference
> She is a woman, heaven knows,
> What is the difference? It isn't only the sex,
> It's the way that love loves, over the walls, despite
>     armor, after the end of the world,
> But I don't know how to say it.
> I hear the alto wondering who
> Her vast clear night full of tears
> Trembles soprano and falters up there

And falls again
And at once regains breath and escapes all my questions
  that hold me below.
Higher up, the questions don't follow, there are only
  answers
Which is why women's voices are so joyful and free.

The word "woman" holds me captive. I would like to wear it out, to lose it, and to continue along on the trail of She who lives without this great worry.

All the more lovable for being more woman all the more man for being more woman and perhaps all the more woman . . .

If I loved a woman, I would call her with my voice still moist and salty, Tancredi my Beloved.

# 4

## *The Last Painting or the Portrait of God*

I would like to write like a painter. I would like to write like painting.

The way I would like to live. Maybe the way I manage to live, sometimes. Or rather: the way it is sometimes given to me to live, in the present absolute.

In the happening of the instant.

Just at the moment of the instant, in what unfurls it, I touch down then let myself slip into the depth of the instant itself.

This is how I live, this is how I try to write. The best company for me is she or he who is in touch with the instant, in writing.

And what is a painter? A bird-catcher of instants.

"I will have to work very hard to render what I am looking for: the instantaneous impression, particularly the envelope of things, the same all-pervading light."[1]

Monet, in 1890, is the one who said that: what I am looking for, instantaneousness . . . the same light spread throughout, the same light, the same light.

There is a literary *oeuvre* which is dear to me, the work of Clarice Lispector. She wrote *Agua Viva*. This book aims to write-paint, aims to work on the gesture of writing as a gesture of painting. I say "aims": one can always ask oneself the question of the reality of the thing. What brings this book closer to a painter's gesture is that it is a book of instants, a book from which each page could be taken out like a picture. Clarice says: "Each thing has an instant in which it is. I want to take possession of the thing's *is*."[2]

I want to take hold of the third person of the present. For me, that is what painting is, the chance to take hold of the third person of the present, the present itself.

But in life, it is "only in the act of love—by the clear, starlike abstraction of what one feels [that] we capture the unknown quality of the instant, which is hard and crystalline and vibrant in the air, and life is that incalculable instant, greater than the event itself."

Who could write: "Is my theme the instant? my life theme. I try to keep up with it, I divide myself thousands of times, into as many times as the seconds that pass away, fragmentary as I am and precarious the moments."[3] It may be Clarice Lispector, it may be Monet.

I would like to write to what is living in life; I would like to be in the sea and render it in words. Which is impossible. I would like to write the rose-colored beach and the pearly ocean. And it is February. Completely impossible. My words can't tell you the simultaneously infinite and yet finite beach rolled out like a immense carpet of rosy sands. My words are colorless. Barely sonorous? What I can tell you, a painter would show you.

I would like to break your heart with the magnificent calm of a beach safe from man. But I can't do it, I can only tell it. All I can do is tell the desire. But the painter can break your heart with the epiphany of a sea. There's a recipe: "To really paint the sea, you have to see it everyday, at every hour and in the same place, to come to know the life in this location."[4]

That's Monet. Monet who knows how to paint the sea: how to paint the sameness of the sea.

It's in vain that I say to you: Côte Rocheuse, Lion's Rock, Belle-Ile. And the green sea and the black lion don't fall on your heart over and over. I tell you of the rocks at Belle-Ile. But eternity doesn't suddenly stream forth and enter, weeping, through your eyes into the depths of your body.

With a haystack, I tell you "haystack," I don't reveal the setting sun to you, I don't intoxicate you with the discovery of the colors in the light, I don't make you laugh, I don't make you cry. I write.

I love paintings the way the blind must love the sun: feeling it, breathing it in, hearing it pass through the trees, adoring it with regret and pain, knowing it through the skin, seeing it with the heart. I don't paint. I need painting. I write in the direction of painting. I position myself toward the sun. Toward the light. Toward painting.

The blind don't see the sun? They see the sun in a different way. And perhaps I, in writing, paint in a different way. I paint in the dark. But this is my blind way of calling forth light.

I'm calling.

There are mimosas in the garden. I want so much to give them to you to see.

I am only a poet, I am only a poor painter without canvas without brush without palette.

But not without God; being only a poet, I am really obligated to count on God, or on you, or on someone.

I'm calling: Mimosa! I'm calling you.

I tell you on the telephone: I want so much for you to see the mimosas. I send you the word "mimosa;" I hope that once delivered to your breast, it will transform itself into a vision of mimosa. I am a being who paints mimosas by phone.

If I were a painter! I would give you each mimosa-cluster whole. I would give you my mimosa-soul, down to the most minute quivering of the yellow spheres.

I would put my mimosoul on the canvas, before your eyes. But I don't paint. I can only speak to you of mimosas. I can sing the word "mimosa." I can make the magic name ring out, the mimosa word: I can give you the music of the mimosa. I can swear to you that (the) mimosa is a synonym for alleluia.

And still, how fortunate that there is the word "mimosa"! I can tell you that the mimosa mimes. I can tell you, too, that the mimosa originates in Brazil.

But I can't nourish your eyes with mimosa light. So I beg you: please, see the mimosas that I see. Imagine the mimosas. See what you don't see, out of love for me. The mimosa is the painter's nymph.

I am the awkward sorceress of the invisible: my sorcery is powerless to evoke, without the help of your sorcery. Everything I evoke depends on you, depends on your trust, on your faith.

I gather words to make a great straw-yellow fire, but if you don't put in your own flame, my fire won't take, my words won't burst into pale yellow sparks. My words will remain dead words. Without your breath on my words, there will be no mimosas.

Ah! If I were Monet. I would fill your house with mimosas, with wisteria, with poppies. With palm trees. With straw. Only their fragrance would be missing.

I write. But I need the painter to give a face to my words. First of all, I write; then you must paint what I've said to you.

Am I jealous of the painter's power? Yes. No. I sense the terrific beating of the painter's heart, the vertigo, the urgency. It is perhaps what I like the most in painting: the beating of the heart. If I were a painter, what pain! what passion! What incessant jealousy of the sky, of the air, what torturous adoration of the light! If I were a painter I would see, I would see, I would see, I would see, I would be panic-stricken, I would run incessantly toward the potato fields, toward the pollard willows. If I were a painter I would know immediately that America is in the heath.

Since I am not a painter, I make detours and go through texts: "Do come and paint with me on the heath, in the potato field, come and walk with me behind the plough and the shepherd—come and sit with me, looking into the fire—let the storm that blows across the heath blow through you.

"Break loose from your bonds. I do not know the future, in what way it might be different if everything should go smoothly with us, but I cannot speak differently: Don't seek it in Paris, don't seek it in America; it is always the same, forever and ever exactly the same. Change, if you will, but it is in the heath you must look."[5]

That was Van Gogh.

I would roll around in desire and pain if I were a painter beneath the stars; if I were a painter I would die endlessly of wonder. I would live in ecstasy until it was at last granted to me to *no longer* see the stars, to no longer see the silk of gray-silver water crossed through and through by a fine strip of sun from my feet to the infinite, in the water, to no longer see the magnificence of sun-powder, until it was at last granted to me to stretch myself out in the dust, to rest among the marvelous powders of the earth. If I were a painter I would live in the fire, I would want to take up the fire in my hands. I would want to catch fire. I would end up losing my sight, and I would thank God. It's fitting that Monet painted with eyes closed, at the end of his life.

I am nearsighted. And even if I have often blamed God for this, I often thank him for it. It's a relief. My nearsightedness spares me the agony of those who see the secrets of the sky. I write because I am nearsighted: it's also, I think, through nearsightedness, thanks to my nearsightedness, that I love:

I am someone who looks at things from very, very close up. Seen through my eyes, little things are very big. Details are my kingdoms. Some people survey. Some people who are far-seeing don't see what is very near. I am someone who sees the smallest letters of the earth. Flat on my stomach in the garden, I see the ants, I see each of the ants' feet. Insects become my heroes. Am I not a little bit right? Human beings are divine insects.

What is beautiful is that such little creatures can be so big.

Such are the benefits of my nearsightedness. This is how I console myself for not being a painter. Would I love this way if I were a painter?

How do I sense what I don't know—the painter's agony? The paintings are what tell me about the painter's passion.

Not just *one* singular painting. But rather a series, a sheaf of paintings, a herd of paintings, a flock, a tribe of paintings. I see Monet's twenty-six cathedrals. I don't know if *one* cathedral would carry me away. Twenty-six cathedrals is a full gallop.

And I sense the struggle. I see the race of speed with the light. I see the challenge. I see the audacity.

The painter is the combatant of enigma.

The painter, the true painter, doesn't know how to paint. He looks for the secret. He will put his life into it. The painter is always Percival. He sets off, he leaves the forest, but in order to come back, on his way around the world, to the forest. I sense the painter's superhuman task: to capture the hundred cathedrals that are born in one day from the cathedral of Rouen. To see them being born. To see them succeeding one another. To see the cathedral in all its lights in one hour. It's to die for.

So he attacks the cathedral and the cathedral attacks him.

This is the struggle with the cathedral: "It's killing, and for this I give up everything, you, my garden . . . And something which never happens, my sleep was filled with nightmares: the cathedral fell down on top of me, it appeared either blue, pink or yellow."[6] And Julie Manet tells us: "Mr. Monet showed us his cathedrals. There are twenty-six of them, and they are magnificent. Some are entirely violet, others white and yellow, with a blue sky, or pink with a slightly green sky. Then there is one in the fog . . . You discover every detail in them; they are as if suspended in mid-air."[7]

Seeing the cathedral's truth which is twenty-six, and noting it, means seeing time. Painting time. Painting the marriage of time with light. Painting the works of time and light.

That's what I would like to do if I were a painter.

The sun moves so quickly. The cathedral changes so often. It was pink a short time ago. Now look at it, violet and flying low.

And we are so slow.

Life is so rapid.

"I doggedly keep exploring a series of different effects (of haystacks), but at this time of year the sun goes down so quickly that I cannot follow it."[8]

Following the sun, painting the differences. I see Monet attacking his poppy field, mounted on four easels. The paintbrushes fly about. Monet is racing.

And even as I have been writing this page, the sun has disappeared. We who write are so slow. And I think of the painter's magic swiftness.

Writing this, I said to myself that perhaps what I like about painting is its mad speed. And people will tell me, there are also slow painters. I don't know. I know nothing about it. I only imagine. But only those who are fast, those who pursue haystacks on four easels, matter to me.

And I think of the rapidity and fatality of desire: vying with light. "You need a Japanese swiftness." No, that wasn't Hokusai, but Van Gogh.

While I was writing this, I prudently held myself back from going out into all the fields that surround me, in order to avoid a too-great vertigo, and it was only when this brief reflection was over that I rewarded myself and wanted to reread Van Gogh's letters. I had been convinced that Van Gogh was a slow painter. Here is what I found:

The Japanese draw quickly, very quickly, like a lightning flash, because their nerves are finer, their feeling simpler.

. . . I have only been here a few months, but tell me this— could I, in Paris, have done the drawing of the boats *in an hour?* Even without the perspective frame, I do it now without measuring, just by letting my pen go.[9]

It is great that Claude Monet managed to paint those ten pictures between February and May. Quick work doesn't mean less serious work, it depends on one's self-confidence and experience.[10]

I must warn you that everyone will think that I work too fast. Don't you believe a word of it.

Is it not emotion, the sincerity of one's feeling for nature, that draws us, and if the emotions are sometimes so strong that one works without knowing one works, when sometimes the strokes come with a continuity and a coherence like words in a speech or a letter, then one must remember that it has not always been so, and that in time to come there will again be hard days, empty of inspiration.

So one must strike while the iron is hot, and put the forged bars on one side.

I have not yet done half the 50 canvases fit to be shown in public, and I must do them all this year.

I know beforehand that they will be criticized as *hasty.*

. . . If my health doesn't betray me, I shall polish off my canvases, and there will be some that will do among them.[11]

And to do that, what lightness must have been achieved!

For that, one has to have broken off with everything that holds one back: calculations, backward or sideways glances, hidden motives, acquired, accumulated, hardened knowledge. And especially all the fears: fear of the unknown, fear of criticism, fear of not knowing, fear of the evil eye: "They will say I am mad" (that's Monet). Fears, one shakes them off. One plays with them. One paints quicker than they take hold.

One does not paint yesterday, one does not even paint today, one paints tomorrow, one paints what will be, one paints "the imminence of."

And to do that, letting go of all ties, one flings oneself beyond the ego. This is perhaps the greatest lesson painting gives us: flinging oneself beyond the ego. For the ego is the last root preventing flight. Or the last anchor. One has to unfasten oneself the best one can, with a snap, or by slowly filing away the soul-ring of lead.

I imagine it's easier for a landscape painter than for a writer to get free; the charm of the visible world is so powerful. At times, the painter's ego is no more attached than a milk tooth. A pull, and straight away, with a leap, in the middle of creation. We are born together. It's raining. We know nothing. We are part of everything.

"Under this fine rain I breathe in the innocence of the world. I feel coloured by the nuances of infinity. At this moment I am at one with my picture. We are an iridescent chaos . . . The sun penetrates me soundlessly like a distant friend that stirs up my laziness, fertilises it. We bring forth life."[12]

That was Cézanne.

At that moment, when the ego no longer weighs him down, the painter becomes permeable, becomes immense and virgin, and becomes woman. He lets light work in him. Submission to the process. He becomes tender, he becomes plant, he becomes earth, the sun impregnates him. *Tanta mansidão,* such gentleness . . . [13]

But how do we obtain this lightness, this active passivity,

this capacity to let things come through, this submission to the process? We who are so heavy, so obstinately activist, so impatient. How could we become virgin and young and innocent? How could we come all the way from our over-furnished memories and our museums of words to the garden of beginnings and rustlings?

This is our problem as writers. We who must paint with brushes all sticky with words. We who must swim in language as if it were pure and transparent, though it is troubled by phrases already heard a thousand times. We who must clear a new path with each thought through thickets of clichés. We who are threatened at every meta-phor, as I am at this moment, with false steps and false words.

But there is a path. It makes us go around the world to regain the second innocence. It's a long path. Only at the end of the path can we regain the force of simplicity or of nudity. Only at the end of life, I believe, will we be able to understand life's secret. One must have traveled a great deal to discover the obvious. One must have thoroughly rubbed and exhausted one's eyes in order to get rid of the thousands of scales we start with from making up our eyes.

There are poets who have strived to do this. I call "poet" any writing being who sets out on this path, in quest of what I call the second innocence, the one that comes after knowing, the one that no longer knows, the one that knows how not to know.

I call "poet" any writer, philosopher, author of plays, dreamer, producer of dreams, who uses life as a time of "approaching." Fortunately, we have inherited rigorous accounts of their adventures. There are poet-painters, like Van Gogh. There are poet-painters like Clarice Lispector.

Whoever would like to know how to go about clearing the gaze should read *The Passion According to G.H.*,[14] by Clarice Lispector.

One must have gone a long way in order to finally leave behind our need to veil, or lie, or gild. Leaving behind the need to gild: this would be the passion according to Rembrandt.

In his very beautiful texts on Rembrandt, Genet says (still remaining within the tradition of reading Rembrandt) that the trajectory of Rembrandt's works began by gilding, by covering over with gold, and then by burning the gold, consuming it, to attain the gold-ash with which the last paintings are painted.

It is only at the end of a superhuman human-going-to-the-depths-of-the-fathoming-of-life-and-back that one will be able to cease gilding everything (Rimbaud and Clarice also knew this). And then one can begin to adore.

This is when one will be allowed to arrive at what I have called, in a text entitled *Lemonade Everything Was So Infinite,* "the last phrase," the one that holds on to the book or the author with no more than a breath. I have allowed myself to adventure toward the canvas partly because I had written this text, *Lemonade Everything Was So Infinite.* Because, in order to work on what is, for me, the very treasure of writing—in other words, ultimate phrases that are full of being, both so heavy and so light that they are more precious to me than an entire book; in order to work on the mystery of these phrases, I have been led to help myself with painting. I have not found any other more helpful example than some of the long journeys undertaken by painters, by Rembrandt in particular. And, arbitrarily or not, I had made a distinction between what I had called "works of art" and "works of being." For me, works of art are works of seduction, works that can be magnificent, works that are really destined to make themselves seen. Where I am arbitrary is in classifying this or that painter in this or that category. For example, for me, da Vinci's works are only works of art. This may be a mistake. But I will put forward a hypothesis: let us look at a painting by da Vinci and a painting by Rembrandt. We will see da Vinci's painting search us out with its eyes, not take its eyes off us, catch hold of us: these are eye-catching paintings.

In Rembrandt, what is overwhelming is the extent to which in the most intense presence, the people he has looked at are alone, have the absence of intimacy, do not feel themselves looked at; they are looking inside their hearts in the direction of the infinite. By going along this double path, I am now able to tell myself that what matters to me most, in art, are works of being: works which no longer need to proclaim their glory, or their magisterial origin, to be signed, to return, to make a return to celebrate the author. This was why, in the text where I dealt with that topic, I inscribed like a precious stone the phrase: "Lemonade everything was so infinite . . . ," a phrase that signified everything to me, the beginning and the end, the whole of life, enjoyment, nostalgia, desire, hope—an *unsigned* phrase by Kafka, a phrase that fell from his hand, from his man's hand at the moment he was not striving to be a writer, the moment he was Franz Kafka himself, beyond books. If these phrases have been collected and printed in spite of everything, it is because it was God's will that, deprived of his voice, as he was dying, Kafka scribbled down, on scraps of paper, what was passing through his mind: and those who were with him at the moment of his passing collected those scraps of paper that are for me the most beautiful books in the world. Perhaps these so very delicate phrases, these phrases of a dying man, are the equivalent, extremely rare in writing, of what is much more frequent in painting: the last paintings. It's at the end, at the moment when one has attained the period of relinquishing, of adoration, and no longer of gilding, that miracles happen.

A magnificent thing happened to Hokusai:

In loving the pretentious style of He-ma-mu-sho-Niūdō, the painter Yamamizu Tengu, of Noshi-Koshiyama, appropriated for himself the incomprehensible art of his drawings. Now, I who have studied this style for almost a hundred years, without understanding any more of it than he, nevertheless had this strange thing happen to me: I notice that my characters, my animals, my insects, my fish, look as if they are escaping from the paper. Is this not truly extraordinary? And a publisher, who was informed of this fact, asked for these drawings, in such a way that I could not refuse him. Fortunately the engraver Ko-Izumi, a very skilled woodcutter, with his very sharp knife, took care to cut the veins and nerves of the beings I drew, and was able to deprive them of the liberty of escaping.[15]

What we have, when Hokusai was over two hundred years old, at the time when he was finally five or six years old, is a collection of drawings that scarcely hold back the beings, fish, insects, or men within their narrow limits.

In what way can I feel close to the painter (the one I love, the madman of painting, of drawing, the unworldly, the celestial, the airborne, the burning)?

First of all, in the need not to lie, not to veil in writing. Which doesn't mean I manage not to lie. It's so difficult not to lie when one writes. And maybe even in the need to write in order to lie less, to scrape the scales away, the too-rich words, to undecorate, unveil. In the need not to submit the subject of writing, of painting, to the laws of cultural cowardice and habit.

In the need, which doesn't mean its execution, not to make things pretty, not to make things clean, when they are not; not to do the right thing. But, whatever the price, to do the true thing.

Rembrandt, who is said not to have had particularly audacious tendencies, but who as a painter was absolutely free, drew and painted nude women I find admirably beautiful, although not everyone has been of this opinion. Here is what a contemporary, A. Houbraken, said in 1710:

Rembrandt . . . refused to conform to the rules of other artists, and still less to follow the illustrious examples of those who had covered themselves with glory by taking beauty as a model; he contented himself with representing life as it offered itself to him, without making a choice. This is why the great poet Andries Pels very wittily said of him in his *Use and Abuse of the Stage* (page 36): "Whenever he had to paint a nude woman, he took as a model not a Greek Venus but rather a washerwoman or servant girl from an inn: he called this deviation the imitation of nature and treated all the rest as vain decoration. From the sagging breasts and the deformed hands, to the frayed lace of the bodice opening across the stomach, to the garters around the legs—everything had to be shown, in order to remain faithful to nature. He did not want to listen to any of the rules of moderation that recommended the representation of only certain parts of the body."

I greatly appreciate Pels's frankness and I ask the reader not to misinterpret my sincere opinion: I do not hate the work of this man, but I wish to compare the different conceptions and methods of art, and to incite those who desire to learn to follow the best way. Apart from this, I join the same poet in saying: "What a loss for art that such a skilled hand did not use its gifts better! For who would have surpassed him? But the greater the genius, the more he can stray when he does not yield to any principles or to any traditional rule, and when he thinks he can find everything within himself."[16]

And to think that today, in our time, people think like this self-righteous biographer, but with a slight difference: painters are allowed to contemplate a woman's real nudity. But in writing, this is not yet entirely allowed.

What does my gesture of writing have in common with the gesture of the one who paints?

The concern with fidelity. Fidelity to what exists. To everything that exists. And fidelity is equal respect for what *seems* beautiful to us and what *seems* ugly to us. I stress *seems*.

But under the paintbrush, before the gaze, in the light of respect, there is nothing ugly which does not seem equally beautiful.

Painting does not know the ugly.

It isn't the beautiful that is true. It's the true that is . . . I don't want to say beautiful. The ugly looked at with respect and without hatred and without disgust is equal to the "beautiful." The nonbeautiful is also beautiful.

Or rather, there is no beautiful more beautiful than the ugly. In painting as in writing, there is no other "beauty" than fidelity to what is. Painting renders—but what it renders is justice. Everything that is: the cathedral, the hay-stack, the sunflowers, the vermin, the peasants, the chair, the skinned ox, the flayed man, the cockroach.

Because everything that is loved, everything that finds grace, is equal to the "beautiful." Everything we don't reject.

We are the ones who decide that this is beautiful, that this is ugly. With our selfish tastes and distastes.

But everything is equal to God and to the painter. And this lesson is often given to the poet by painting. To love the ugly with an equal-to-equal love.

Everything that is (looked at justly) is good. Is exciting. Is "terrible." Life is terrible. Terribly beautiful, terribly cruel. Everything is marvelously terrible, to whoever looks at things as they are.

"I am toiling away at the rate of six paintings a day. I find it *terribly* difficult to catch all the colours of this country; at times, I am *appalled* at the kind of colours I have to use, I'm afraid my colours will seem *terrible* and yet I have consid-erably toned them down: this place is *drenched in light . . .* But how happy I am here because each day I can find the same effect again, *catch it and come to grips with it.*"[17]

That was Monet.

Seeing the world as it is demands strengths, virtues. Which ones? Patience and courage.

The patience one has to have to approach the nonosten-sible, the minute, the insignificant, to discover the worm as a star without luster. To discover the grasshopper's worth.

The patience one must have to see the egg. The egg that might bore us at first glance the way a stone would. One needs patience to contemplate the egg, to brood on it, to see the hen in the egg, to see the history of the world in this shell. One needs another patience to see the absolute egg, the egg without the hen, the egg without signs, the naked egg, the egg egg. And it is with this patience that we can hope to see God.

And the kind of courage?

The greatest kind of courage. The courage to be afraid. To have the two fears. First we have to have the courage to be afraid of being hurt. We have to not defend ourselves. The world has to be suffered. Only through suffering will we know certain faces of the world, certain events of life: the courage to tremble and sweat and cry is as necessary for Rembrandt as for Genet. And it is necessary for Clarice Lispector to have the courage to feel disgust and love for the beggar with the amputated leg, disgust and love for the stump, horror at the rat which is also acceptance of the rat. For whoever writes, accepting the rat demands a far greater effort than for whoever has accepted the rat in advance, has begun to paint it. Whoever writes can easily hide her eyes.

And there is also the other fear, the least dazzling, the most burning: the fear of reaching joy, acute joy, the fear of allowing oneself to be carried away by exaltation, the fear of adoring. We must not be afraid of feeling this fear scalding the blood in our veins.

I am talking about what we are given to see, the spectacle of the world. Maybe it's easier for a painter than for someone who writes not to create hierarchies.

Painting may be more adept at not forgetting turtles than writing is. Writing is terribly human. Perhaps the word causes more fear and more hurt? . . . I don't know.

We can say joy. Can we paint it?

I'm talking about fidelity.

But perhaps the rarest, the most magnanimous fidelity, is the one we could have with regard to the reality of the human soul. It is so hard not to hate! Not to be the wolf for the other. To have for the traitor or the villain, the executioner, Rembrandt's calm and tender eyes for those who loved him, for those who betrayed him. Could Rembrandt be Shakespeare? I thought about it, thinking it was an impertinence. Van Gogh had thought about it before me.

I have already read *Richard II, Henry IV* and half of *Henry V*. I read without wondering if the ideas of the people of those times were different from our own, or what would become of them if you confronted them with republican and socialist beliefs and so on. But what touches me, as in some novelists of our day, is that the voices of these people, which in Shakespeare's case reach us from a distance of several centuries, do not seem unfamiliar to us. It is so much alive that you think you know them and see the thing.

And so what Rembrandt has alone or almost alone among painters, that tenderness of gaze which we see, whether it's in the "Men of Emmaus" or in the "Jewish Bride" or in some strange angelic figure as the picture you have had the good fortune to see, that brokenhearted tenderness, that glimpse of a superhuman infinitude that seems so natural there—in many places you come upon it in Shakespeare too. And then above all he is full of portraits, grave or gay, like "Six" and the "Traveler," and like "Saskia."[18]

That was Van Gogh shortly before his death.

To be faithful as Shakespeare was to Lady Macbeth, to King Lear, to Shylock.

To create without commentary, without condemnation, without interpretation.

With respect for the shadows as for the light. Without knowing more or better.

I envy the painter: humility, in other words the justice of the look, is more easily granted to him than to the one who writes; because the painter is always defeated. He sees himself defeated. He always emerges out of breath from the combat that throws him on the world. Doesn't he always have before him the painting he hasn't done? The twenty-seventh cathedral, to remind him that one cathedral will always have escaped him?

Doesn't he have before his eyes the painting he will not do, the one that slips by his brush? The one he will do tomorrow, tomorrow if God wills it, or never?

There are painters who for me are voyagers of truth. They have given me lessons.

Whom do I call the voyagers of truth?

The one who painted water lilies for the last ten years of his life. The one who painted water lilies up until the last painting. Until his death. And then: "The sea: I should like to always be before it or above it, and when I am dead, to be buried in a buoy."[19] That is Monet's wish—to become seagull, water lily.

The one who painted a hundred Fujiyamas. The one who signed the map of China: "Old man Manji crazy about painting, voyager from Katsushika, eighty-one years old."

The one who searches until the last painting.

The one who paints with his right hand, his left hand, with his nails. This is Hokusai.

The one who knows that he will not find, because he knows that if he found, he would have nothing else to do except continue to search for the new mystery. The one who knows he must continue to search.

The one who does not become discouraged, does not tire.

I love the one who dares to stalk the secrets of light with the help of a single subject, armed with only a few water lilies.

And the lesson is: one does not paint ideas. One does not paint "a subject." One does not paint water lilies. And in the same way: no writing ideas. There is no subject. There are only mysteries. There are only questions.

Kandinsky sees the haystacks: "And suddenly, for the first time, my eyes were drawn to a painting . . . I had the confused feeling that the subject was lacking in this picture . . . The subject, as the necessary element of paintings, lost all credit to my eyes."[20]

What a struggle to no longer "paint water lilies," while *painting* water lilies. I mean: in order not to do the portrait of the water lilies, what a number of water lilies he will have had to paint before the representation of the water lilies wears itself out, before the water lilies are no longer the cause, before they are no longer the object, the aim, but the occasion, the everyday water lily, the day itself, the day's atom on the canvas.

Until they are no more, these water lilies, than Hokusai's everyday lion. In 1843, at the age of eighty-three, Hokusai tells himself that it is time he did his lions, and every morning he does his karashishi: "I continue to draw hoping for a peaceful day"—that was the way he did two hundred nineteen of them, until the lions were no more than the water lilies' path toward infinity.

And how I love the one who dared to paint the painter, again and again, until at the hundredth "self-portrait" he succeeded in painting the painter impersonally; and yet ever so humanly, so nakedly human. Until we no longer think, "This is a portrait of Rembrandt by himself." Until at the hundredth portrait the name is so worn out that it no longer hides the man at all. And this man is as he is. He is old and absent-minded and, without proclaiming it and perhaps without knowing it, full of the mystery of age, time, and death.

I was in England during the Second World War, without any money and unhappy. My wife, who is younger and more courageous than I, said to me: "Let's go and look for consolation in a museum." Ruins were accumulating on the face of the earth. Not only was London being bombed—which was of little importance—but we learned every day of the annihilation of a new city. Devastation, destruction: the annihilation of a world becoming poorer and sadder. What bitterness. I looked at the last self-portrait of Rembrandt: ugly and broken, dreadful and full of despair; and so marvelously painted. And suddenly I understood: being capable of looking at oneself disappearing into the mirror —no longer seeing anything—and painting oneself as "nothingness," the negation of man. What a miracle, what a symbol. I drew courage and a new youth from this.[21]

That was Kokoschka.

How much patience, how much time in order for Rembrandt to cease resembling Rembrandt, to cease clinging to Rembrandt, and little by little to let himself slide, without being frightened, into the resemblance of someone, of no one.

How much greater a love for painting than for oneself! To come as far as the portraits of a man who allows himself to look, who allows himself to paint, who gives himself to be painted, by renouncing himself, who gives himself to painting as others do to God. And as the dead man does to science. So that it can advance on his body.

Perhaps Rembrandt dreamed of doing the last portrait of

the painter? The one that only Rembrandt, at the end of his life, could have done? I dream of it.

The portrait of Rembrandt on his deathbed? For it is at this moment that he would have perceived the most anonymous, the most present, the most immediate, the most ephemeral, the essential, the mystery of human being. And if almost dead or already dead, in other words entirely freed from the rest of the Rembrandt he had painted, then he would have painted painting itself. He would truly have painted like no one.

I dream of this purity. I dream of this power of freedom. To paint the enigma. The enigmatic in painting. I think of the last Rembrandt. A man? Or a painting? I think of the last Hokusai. What is the name of the person who painted the last Hokusai?

I think of Hokusai's series of names like the series of water lilies. He had a hundred and one names. First he was called Shunro. Then, expelled from school, took the name Kusamara. Took the name Sori in '95. Hokusai Sori-ga, which means Studio of the North Star, Source of Truth; also called himself Toito, Litsu, Zen Hokusai, Gakyojin Hokusai, then Tawaraya, Hyakurin, Kanchi, and Sori.

Then abandoned the name Sori to his pupil. And called himself Tatsumasa, Sorobeku, Tokitaro, Gayojin Totogako Zen Hokusai, Sensei Kutsushika Taito, Zen Hokusai Tasmeitsu Gakyorojin Manji. All these names had a meaning. Not one was Hokusai.

Following himself without turning back. One after the other letting himself go.

Always being the future. Being the follower. The next one. Being one's own next one. The unknown one. Surpassing oneself. And yet not preceding the self. Abandoning oneself. In words. In curves. Abandoning one's names. One's signatures. Giving oneself entirely to rediscovery.

And so, in the course of time, what does this produce? What does this produce in the end?

A possibly mad purity.

One can tell the facts. One can invent some. It is more difficult to tell than to invent. Inventing is easy.

But the most difficult is fidelity to what one feels, there, at the extremity of life, at the nerve endings, around the heart.

And for that, there are no words. For what one feels, there are no words. For the reality of the soul, there are no words. But there are tears. One can allude to the divine. But the word "god" is only a subterfuge.

Words are our accomplices, our traitors, our allies. We have to make use of them, spy on them, we should be able to purify them.

This is the dream of philosophers and poets. Words drive us mad. "By repeating a word over and over again, it loses its meaning and becomes a hollow and redundant thing, and attains its own hard, enigmatic body."[22]

Clarice amused herself by saying, "Spirit, spirit, spirit." And in the end, spirit flew. In the end, what is spirit?

"It is a sparkling and audacious word, like a flight of sparrows. Sometimes the repeated word becomes the dry orange-skin of itself, and no longer glows with even a sound."[23]

What happens at the end of two hundred nineteen lions? What happens at the end of ten thousand or a hundred thousand water lilies?

I claim the right to repeat the word until it becomes dry orange-skin, or until it becomes fragrance. I want to repeat the words "I love you" until they become spirit.

But repetition, in those who write, is very badly received. The painter has the right to repeat until water lilies become divine sparrows.

To practice abandoning oneself to the water lilies.

Perhaps in the end that would give the portrait of God, or the self-portrait of God by Hokusai.

When Hokusai produced the hundred views of Mount Fuji, this is what he said:

From the age of six, I had a passion for drawing the form of objects. By the age of about fifty, I had published an infinity of drawings, but nothing I produced before the age of seventy is worth counting. It was at the age of seventy-three that I more or less understood the structure of true nature, of animals, grasses, birds, fish, and insects.

Consequently, by the age of eighty, I will have made even more progress; at ninety I will penetrate the mystery of things; at a hundred I will definitely have reached a degree of wonder, and when I am a hundred and ten, for my part, be it a.dot, be it a line, everything will be alive.

I ask those who will live as long as I do to see if I keep my word.

Written at the age of seventy-five by myself, formerly Hokusai, today Gwakiō Rōjin, the old man crazy about drawing.[24]

This is truly the message of hope. It gives me a great deal of hope; I tell myself that when I am a hundred and ten, I will likewise know how to write a book that will be a dot.

Painting and writing—they are just that, hoping absolutely, they are what we might call *sunflower life,* to borrow an image from Van Gogh or from Clarice Lispector: "Almost all lives are small. What enlarges a life is the inner life, are the thoughts, are the sensations, are the useless hopes . . . Hope is like a sunflower which turns aimlessly toward the sun. But it is not 'aimless.' "[25]

What enlarges a person's life are the impossible dreams, the unrealizable desires. The one that has not yet come true. And these hopes, these desires are so strong that at times one falls, and when a person falls, she sees, she is once again turned toward the inaccessible sun. Why does the flower have a fragrance that is not for anyone, and for nothing . . .

Like hope. Hope aims at hope itself.

And the painter? Paints from hope to hope. And between the two? Is there despair? Nonhope. Between-hope. But straightaway, hope arises. What I love is the painter's dissatisfaction, what a wonder: a furious Monet burning thirty canvases. Destroying his "overworked" canvases.

Seen by us, these canvases were "beautiful." Seen by him, they are obstacles on the path to the last one.

His dissatisfaction is hope. Hope for the impossible. To turn oneself once again toward the sun is an act of faith. Writing the sun is as impossible as painting the air. This is what I want to do.

When I have finished writing, when I am a hundred and ten, all I will have done will have been to attempt a portrait of God. Of the God. Of what escapes us and makes us wonder. Of what we do not know but feel. Of what makes us live. I mean our own divinity, awkward, twisted, throbbing, our own mystery—we who are lords of this earth and do not know it, we who are touches of vermilion and yellow cadmium in the haystack and do not see it, we who are the eyes of this world and so often do not even look at it, we who could be the painters, the poets, the artists of life if only we wanted to; we who could be the lovers of the universe, if we really wanted to use our hands with mansuetude, we who so often use our booted feet to trample the world's belly.

We who are bits of sun, drops of ocean, atoms of the god, and who so often forget this, or are unaware of it, and so we take ourselves for employees. We who forget we could also be as luminous, as light, as the swallow that crosses the summit of the incomparable hill Fuji, so intensely radiant that we could ourselves be the painter's models, the heroes of human presence and the painter's gaze. But what we forget, the painter, who sees God each day in the process of changing, does not forget . . .

In what way do I feel different from these painters I love? In my way of loving an interior apple as much as an exterior apple.

"I received today a splendid apple, sent by Mr. Bellio; by its size and colours it is quite a phenomenon: he tells me that amidst so many orange trees I might feel like biting into a big apple from Normandy, hence his nice present.

"I did not dare to bite into it and offered it to Mr. Moreno."[26]

That was Monet.

Myself, I would have eaten it. In this way, I am different from those I would like to resemble. In my need to touch the apple without seeing it. To know it in the dark. With my fingers, with my lips, with my tongue.

In my need to share with you the food, the bread, the words, the painted food and also the not-painted food.

In my need to make use of my right hand to hold the pen

and write, and of my two hands to hold nothing, to caress and to pray.

I am going to finish . . .

I have a postscript, Hokusai's address. In case, having reached the age of a hundred and ten, we are looking for him, here it is:

"When you come, do not ask for Hokusai; they will not know how to answer you. Ask for the priest who draws and who recently moved into the building, ask the owner Gorobei for the beggar-priest in the courtyard of the Mei-o-in temple, in the middle of the bush."[27]

May I have merited such an address . . . by the time I am ninety years old . . .

# 5

## *By the Light of an Apple*

This woman was almost unbelievable. Or rather: her writing was. Einstein said that someday the world would find it hard to believe that a man like Gandhi had ever existed in flesh and blood on this earth.

With Clarice Lispector we find it difficult, but also wonderful, to believe she could have existed so close to us, just yesterday, and so far ahead of us. Kafka is also irretrievable, except . . . through her.

If Kafka had been a woman. If Rilke had been a Jewish Brazilian born in the Ukraine. If Rimbaud had been a mother, if he had reached the age of fifty. If Heidegger had been able to stop being German, if he had written the Romance of the Earth. Why have I cited these names? To try to sketch out the general vicinity. Over there is where Clarice Lispector writes. There, where the most demanding works breathe, she makes her way. But then, at the point where the philosopher gets winded, she goes on, further still, further than all knowledge. After comprehension, step by step, she plunges trembling into the incomprehensible shuddering depth of the world, the ultrasensitive ear, tensed to take in even the sound of the stars, even the minimal rubbing of atoms, even the silence between two heartbeats. Watchwoman, night-light of the world. She knows nothing. She didn't read the philosophers. And yet sometimes you'd swear you could hear them murmur in her forests. She discovers everything.

All the paradoxical movements of the human passions, the painful marriages of opposites that make up life itself, fear and courage (fear is also a kind of courage), madness and wisdom (one is the other, just as the beauty is the beast), lack and satisfaction, thirst equals water . . . All the secrets are discovered for us, and she hands us, one by one, the thousands of keys to the world.

And also this greatest experience, above all today, which is being-poor by dint of poverty, or by dint of wealth.

Where thought stops thinking in order to become a flight of joy—that is where she writes. Where joy becomes so acute it hurts—that is where this woman hurts us.

And also in the street: a handsome man, an old woman, a little redheaded girl, an ugly dog, a big car, a blindman pass by.

And under the gaze of Clarice Lispector, every event hatches; the ordinary opens up and shows its treasure, which is, precisely, ordinary. And suddenly like a storm—of wind, of gunfire, of teeth: life arrives.

Relentless gaze, laborious voice, writing that works to unbury, unearth, unforget—what? The living: the inexhaustible mysteries of our "inhabitation" of the earth. And how many of them there are! Reigns, species, beings. Everything that exists is to be saved, to be pulled from the forgetfulness that takes the place of daily existence for us. And through this work, everything comes back, everything is returned to us, *equally,* from the most splendid to the most banal, all *equally:* everything that has the right to be named, because it *is.* Chair, star, rose, turtle, egg, little boy . . . : she is maternally concerned with all the species of "children."

Like all the greatest works, this one, for the reader, is apprenticeship, humble and incessant astonishment, and at the same time learning. Reeducation of the soul. This work puts us back in the world-school. The work itself as school and schoolgirl. Because whoever writes doesn't know. Which doesn't prevent writing from creating truth without knowing that it does so, the way we sometimes create light, groping around in the dark and finding the unhoped-for body.

Writing: touching the mystery, delicately, with the tips of the words, trying not to crush it, in order to un-lie.

But don't let this worry you: she also writes stories. A rich young woman encounters a beggar. And in six pages it's the Gospel, or rather Genesis. No, I'm not exaggerating very much.

A woman and a cockroach: these are the protagonists of the drama of Re-cognition called *The Passion According to G.H.* Shall I tell you? She (a woman designated by the initials G.H., or writing), which is to say passion, leaves the maid's room. Leaves a white wall on which the silhouette of a woman is drawn. And she advances. Step by page with a regular gait, steady, up to the final revelation. Each page has the fullness of a book. Each chapter is a land. To be explored. To be surpassed. Each step distances the "I" from its ego. At each step, a wall. Opens up. An error. Unveiled. G.H. meets a cockroach. But there will be no monstrous "Metamorphosis." On the contrary: for G.H. the creature is the real representative of a species that has persevered in its roach-being since prehistory. The morsel of life, horrifying, repugnant, admirable in its resistance to death. Of this body, the body of the other, on which she dares, must, does not want to inflict death, she violently asks the secret of the living, of the prehuman material that does not die. What is life, death? If not a human mental construction, a projection of the ego? Prehuman life does not know death. The passion according to G.H. is this crossing of the shell, of all shells, into the unlimited, neutral, impersonal substance . . . material, unlimited, neutral, impersonal . . .

No, I really haven't told you a thing. You must follow her word by word, in her ascension toward the low. Yes; with her, descending is also climbing.

Could it be that now we are her children?

And now I will descend into the terrestrial stars, glimmering weakly in the book *The Hour of the Star.*

# 6

## The Author in Truth

I have always dreamed about the last text of a great writer. A text written with final energies, the last breath. On the last day before death, the author sits on the edge of the earth, feet light in the infinite air, and looks at the stars. Tomorrow the author will be a star among the stars, a molecule among all the molecules. The last day is beautiful for those who know how to live it, it is one of the most beautiful days of life. On that particular day (I should say days, for the last day can be several days) one sees the world through the eyes of the gods: I am finally going to become a part of the worldly mysteries. Sitting on the edge of the earth, the author is already almost no one. The phrases which come from the heart to the lips are released from the book. They are beautiful like the work, but they will never be published, and before the imminence of the starred silence, they hasten, assemble, and say the essential. They are a sublime farewell to life; not mourning, but acknowledgement. How beautiful you are, O life, they say.

One day I wrote a book called *Lemonade Everything Was So Infinite*[1]—it was a book of meditation on one of Kafka's last phrases, a phrase he wrote down on a sheet of paper, just before his death. During this time he no longer spoke out loud, because of the burning in his throat. A phrase came from that unuttered zone where, mute but distinct, the most essential things are said, minuscule things, infinite things, inexpressible outside in the sharp air, because of their fragility and beauty.

This phrase is *Limonade es war alles so grenzenlos.*[2]

For me this is *The Poem,* the ecstasy and the regret, the very simple heart of life. It is the end. And the end of the end. And the first refreshment.

The ultimate works are brief and burning, like the fire that reaches toward the stars. Sometimes they are only one line. They are works written with extraordinary tenderness. Works of gratitude: for life, for death. For it is also as a result of death and *thanks to* death that we discover the splendor of life. It is death that makes us remember the treasures life contains, with all its living misfortunes and its pleasures.

There is a text like a discreet psalm, a song of thanksgiving to death. This text is called *The Hour of the Star.* Clarice Lispector wrote it when she was already almost no one on this earth. In her place, her immensity, the great night was opening forth. A star smaller than a spider was wandering there. This tiny thing, seen at close range, turned out to be a minute human creature, weighing perhaps thirty kilos. But seen from death, or from the stars, she was as big as anything in the world and as important as anyone very important or without importance on our earth.

This minute and almost imponderable person is called Macabea: the book of Macabea is extremely slender, it looks like a very small notebook. It is one of the greatest books in the world.

This book was written by a weary and passionate hand. In a way, Clarice had already ceased to be an author, to be a writer. It is the last text, the one that comes *after*. After all books. After time. After the self. It belongs to eternity, to this time of before after me, which nothing can interrupt. To this time, to this secret and infinite life of which we are fragments.

*The Hour of the Star* tells the story of a minute fragment of human life. Tells faithfully: minutely fragmentarily.

Macabea is not (only) a character of fiction. She is a speck of dust that got into the author's eye and gave rise to a stream of tears. This book is the stream of tears caused by Macabea. It is also a stream of immense and humble questions which do not even ask for answers: they ask for life. This book asks itself: What is an author? Who is worthy of being Macabea's author?

This "book" murmurs to us: Do the beings who live in a work have a right to the author *they need*?

Macabea needs a very special author. It is out of love for Macabea that Clarice Lispector will create the necessary author.

*The Hour of the Star,* Clarice Lispector's last hour, is a small great book that loves and knows nothing, not even its name. Not even its title, I mean. Is *The Hour of the Star* so illiterate that it doesn't know its name? Doesn't have a title properly speaking, hesitates among several titles. For a "title," it inscribes its hesitation among an infinite number of titles. This book could be named according to the hour:

"The Blame Is Mine—or—The Hour of the Star—or— Let Her Fend for Herself—or—The Right to Shout—CLA- RICE LISPECTOR—As for the Future—or—Blues *Lamento*— or—She Doesn't Know How to Shout—or—A Sense of Loss—or—Whistling in the Dark Wind—or—I Can Do Nothing—or—A Record of Preceding Events—or—A

Teargas-like Story of a Cordel—or—A Discreet Exit by the Back Door."[3]

And could also be named: Clarice Lispector. Or, more exactly: Signed Clarice Lispector. The signature "Clarice Lispector" figures among the possible titles of *The Hour of the Star*. An imitated figure. A facsimile of the original signature. The (reproduced) body of the author's proper name (if Clarice Lispector is the author) may be a title of this book. One of its possible proper names. If one can say that the photograph of the signature of Clarice Lispector is still her proper name. Unless the name Clarice Lispector, in the unfurling of hesitation, has taken on the status of the other proposed titles.

If *The Hour of the Star* came to be called Clarice Lispector, then we could think that the book that follows is a biography of Clarice Lispector. It would be her story, a distanced self-portrait, more distanced from its model than the usual self-portrait.

*Or,* which beats the rhythm of all these titles, is also one of the titles.

So here is a book which, by more than one title, could boast of an exceptional wealth in the matter of titles. But this wealth is ruinous. This many titles is too much. If one can replace another, each one cancels out and is canceled out. Which precisely suits the characters in this narrative. Characters who would have a lot of trouble making a name for themselves, raising themselves to the level of a name. Not that the person with whom this narrative is smitten is a simple example in a uniform series.

It's just that she (the person is a woman) exists only below the level of nomination, of the recording of recognition, to which she doesn't know how to pretend.

She doesn't measure up. Being "called" is already a way of being honored. Of taking oneself for something. And even for someone?

Beginning with its very title, *The Hour of the Star* is already modest, effaced. A kind of "as you wish."

So *a* title? How to choose *a* title? In the world where for better or worse the humble shadow of character extends, choosing is a privilege reserved for the rich. Having to choose is a violence—a martyrdom—for the creature who has never had anything. And who thus wants nothing, and wants everything. For whom choosing a cake is the loss of all the cakes not chosen. Who does not *know* how to choose, for knowing how to choose is a science of rich and free people. So she hesitates and waits. Doesn't choose. You, choose for her and deliver her from the impossible freedom which suddenly subjugates her and threatens to crush her.

Because for Macabea's grain of being, one title is worth as much as another.

One creature is worth as much as another.

Another? The other! Ah, the other, here is the name of the mystery, the name of You, the desired one for whom Clarice Lispector has written—all her books. The other to love. The other who puts love to the test: How to love the other, the strange, the unknown, the not-me-at-all? The criminal, the bourgeoise, the rat, the cockroach? How can a woman love a man? Or another woman?

*The Hour of the Star* vibrates completely with these mysteries.

What follows is a modest meditation on this book which is born of books so that it can totter into our hearts like a child.

Now I am going to change tone, to speak a little more coolly about this divine spark.

*H.C.*

Let us try to imagine what would be for each of us, male and female, the most "other" possible, the strangest creature possible, while nevertheless remaining within the sphere of the recognizable; what is the terrestrial creature that would be the strangest possible and would at the same time "touch" us. Everyone has a personal stranger. For Clarice it was this little bit of life, coming from the *Nordeste* of Brazil. The *Nordeste* has, sadly, become famous: people there are happy when they eat rat. A land where in our own time people die of famine, an occidental India. This person comes from one of the most disinherited places in the world, and for Clarice the problem was to work on what it is to be disinherited, to be without inheritance, such that one is without everything, without memory (though not amnesiac), to be so poor that poverty runs through the whole being: blood-poor, language-poor, and memory-poor. But being born and being poor is not a reduction; it is as if one belonged to another planet, a planet from which there is no means of transport to the planet of culture, of food, of satisfaction.

The *personne* Clarice chose, person and no one, this almost-a-woman, is a woman who is scarcely a woman. But she is so completely scarcely-a-woman that she is perhaps more of a woman than any woman, more immediately. She is so small, so minute, that she is right down to the grassroots level of being, as if she had an almost intimate relationship with the first stirrings of life on earth; she is a blade of grass, and she ends up in the grass, as grass. As a blade of grass, as a slip of a woman, she is situated physically, emotionally, right at the base of genesis, at the beginning and at the end. And so, more immediately than we who are heavy and white, she shows the subtlest elements of what one might call "being-a-woman," because, like extremely poor people, she is attentive and makes us attentive to the insigificances that are our essential riches, and that we have forgotten and repressed with our ordinary riches. When she discovers a desire or an appetite, or when she tastes for the first time in her life a food which for us has become the least tempting, the most ordinary of dishes, for her it is a wonder, a most extraordinary discovery. And her wonder gives us back the lost delicacies. And don't throw away that plastic bottle; it's precious.

In order to speak in the most intimate way possible about this woman that she is not, that we are not, that I am not, and whom probably, as the text tells us at one point, the author must have met by chance in the street on her way to market, it was necessary for Clarice to undergo a superhuman exercise of displacement of all her being, of transformation, of estrangement from herself, to try to approach such a minute and transparent being. And what did she do to become sufficiently self-estranged? What she did—so that it would not be "she"—was to be the most other possible from herself, giving rise to something absolutely remarkable: in this case, the most other possible involved passing into the masculine, *passing by way of a man*. Paradoxical step. So, to approach this almost-woman, one sees in the text how (Clarice)-I has not shaved for several days, has not played football, and so on. "I" goes into the masculine, and this particular masculinity impoverishes her. Going into the masculine is, "I" suggests to us, an impoverishment. But like every process of impoverishment with Clarice Lispector, it is a positive movement, a form of asceticism, a way of bridling a part of pleasure, to attain a strange joy. Moreover, in his turn this man "monasterizes" himself, deprives himself, bows down. Double impoverishment.

The author in question must give some explanation of the necessity for this mitigation. "I" says: no one can talk about my heroine—only a man like me can talk about her, because if it were a "woman-writer," she "would weep soft tears." Sly terms, almost a simulacrum of perfunctory machismo. And yet there is reason in this pretense. Of what troubling, troubled species is the author of this statement, who does not state her sex? This is what gives us a dream to dream in acrobatic steps.

Who is the "man" who writes this text? No. Who is the man who writes this text? No. What sex is the writer who is capable of writing this text? No. What sex, then, am I who can write this text? Or: does the text decide the sex of the author? I mean the sex hidden in the sex, the imaginary sex. Or: who is the author of the author? I mean: who makes the author?

This is what happens to the author who sees him(her)self constrained to ask by an extremely demanding subject: Who am I, who are I, at this very moment? A flight of questions beating two she-wings one black one white one he-r one h-ymn one s-he one (s)he-sitation . . .

Mad is the wo(man) who wants to know who I . . .

But could it be paradoxically true, magically true, the

truth at work in the Metamorphoses, that it is through being, through being transformed into, through being in the process of being, an author with a beard . . .

[his personality is threadbare anyhow, he is not the triumphant author of the mass media, he is at the end of life, he tells us that he has nothing left but writing, nothing but that]

It is as a man in extremity, as a stripped being who gives up all pleasures, including football, that Clarice—no, he—finds the most respectful distance from her little slip of a woman.

And we ask ourselves: Why would this not have been possible as a woman? An "I" answers in Clarice's place: a woman might have felt pity. (The "wept soft tears" is a wonderful period touch.) And pity is not respect. The supreme value is without pity, but a without-pity full of respect. In the first few pages, the author claims the right to be without pity. (I, H.C., trying to escape gender determination, find myself obliged to use the indefinite infinitive.) Pity is deforming, it is paternalistic or babying, it coats over, covers up, and what Clarice Lispector wants to do here is to leave this being naked in her minuscule grandeur.

But—taking a step further—I'm cheating like a Clarice in telling you what I'm telling you: that, yes, a man who does not shave, who is at the end of his life, for whom only writing remains, who has no worldly ambition, who has only love (we need to find this man), could be assured of being without pity. Except that this man is Clarice, and—this is her genius—she tells us so: the text opens with the following dedication:

## DEDICATÓRIA DO AUTOR
### *(Na Verdade Clarice Lispector)*

And after this, the dedication unfurls under the sign of music(s):

### Dedication By The Author
### (In Truth Clarice Lispector)

And here I am dedicating this thing here to old Schumann and his sweet Clara, who today are bones, poor us. I dedicate myself to the color red, very scarlet, like this blood of mine which is that of a man in his prime, and hence I dedicate myself to my own blood. I dedicate myself above all to the gnomes, dwarfs, sylphs and nymphs who inhabit my life. I dedicate myself to the longing for my former poverty, when everything was more somber and honorable, and I had never yet eaten lobster. I dedicate myself to the tempest of Beethoven. To the vibration of the neutral colors of Bach. To Chopin, who softens my bones. To Stravinsky, who has frightened me and with whom I have flown into fire. To *Death and Transfiguration,* where Richard Strauss reveals a fate to me? And above all I dedicate myself to the eves of today and to today, to the transparent veil of Debussy, to Marlos Nobre, etc., to the dodecaphonics, to the bitter cries of the electronics—to all those who have reached unexpected zones in me in a terrifying way, all our prophets of the present time who have predicted me to myself to such a degree that in this very instant I explode into: I.[4]

Here we have all the signs and warnings concerning "the author (in truth Clarice Lispector)." This is a text whose author presents herself discreetly, in the third person between parentheses. The author is not single or simple—there is no real author, only an author suspended between

( ). The author is in reserve—and inasmuch as she is true, the truth is reserved. Being an author in truth is being in reserve. On the side. Text not without reserve. Rich in truth, but obliquely.

Clarice Lispector the author on the cover (of the book) is the truth of this author, but like any truth she is kept secret, guarded unknowable. But could she simply slip by us? We know only that she is there like a heart in a breast, we hear her beating the rhythm of life. And what is the truth of Clarice Lispector? (Within this parenthesis another parenthesis opens up, into which gnomes, sylphs, dreams, horses, and creatures of various species precipitate themselves.)

What she is signifying to us here is one of the great mysteries of our existence, and this particular mystery is always too well hidden in real life, seeing that we are all distributed on the stage of life as men and as women, and that we take ourselves for men and women. Now the author (Clarice) says further on in this text, "naming" herself: I alone, "Rodrigo S.M.," can come to love this girl. As for "the girl," she takes name very late in the text, into which she pierces upward like a blade of grass, very slowly. I, Rodrigo S.M., I am in truth Clarice Lispector put in parentheses, and only the author "(in truth Clarice Lispector)" can approach this beginning of a woman. This is the impossible truth. It is *the inexpressible, indemonstrable truth,* which can be said only in parentheses, as a subtitle, set back, among several layers of beings, one working on another; the impossible truth that can't be justified before a philosophical tribunal, can't pass the bar of monological discourses or mass-mediatized imaginations. It is the truth, a woman, beating like a heart, in the parenthesis of life.

The identity of the "I" who cannot answer palpitates inexpressibly at this customs checkpoint, divided into two camps by the human world. Either you understand that or you don't understand it. Either or: there are two universes, and these two universes don't communicate. Either you feel it or you don't. As Clarice says at the end of her dedication, and as she very often says:

"One cannot give a proof of the existence of what is truer, the trick is to believe. *To believe weeping.*"[5]

Is belief a skill, then? Perhaps skill is a question of faith. Yes. It is. Both: it is a matter of taking the leap. Of passing from the kingdom of logic to that of living evidence. Losing assurance to gain truth. In one fell swoop. The trick of faith. The trick: what we have no name for.

Either we believe weeping, and this is when we can inhabit the world where the feminine being and the masculine being come into contact, exchange, caress, and respect each other, are really incapable of keeping up a discourse of exact description of their differences, but live these differences, and where—as the opening of the text tells us—if masculine and feminine get along (I can't say understand each other, because they don't understand each other), it is because there is feminine, and there is masculine, in both. There are obviously points of conjunction, if not of identification.

Or we will not take pleasure in the wealth hidden in this poor book.

It was to evoke this same mystery that I worked on Rossini's *Tancredi*. What interested me in Rossini's *Tancredi* and in the whole line of the Tancredis was the undeveloped mystery, not presented with proofs but instead given to be understood weeping, of the existence of a character all the more man in that he is more woman, just as she is more man in that he is more woman . . . This mystery is easier to convey through music than through writing, because music is not subject as the text is to the fearful imperatives of language that force us to construct sentences with grammatical correctness, to attribute genders properly: writers of fictional texts are called to account. It is in the poem, hybrid of music and language, that something of mysterious and unstoppable life can be produced, with subverted grammar, with liberties in the bosom of language, in the law of genders, in dance, the *dans*(in), the dancing of the poem, minimal world in movement, the poem speaking French, the tongue, very differently from prose, the poem playing with language more than it speaks, chanted expression of drives—but here I am evoking only the poem that invents the other tongue within the tongue, the dream-tongue; only this poem breaks loose from its moorings, spurts from the silence churning with Rimbaud, with Celan, with Mandelstam, with Tsvetaeva . . . smashes the windowpanes . . .

## The Primitive Meal[6]

For the sake of convenience, I have often spoken of "libidinal economies." In order to try to distinguish the vital functions, I say that they exist; but they are not decisively distinguished in reality. In real life traits are effaced, blended together. I have fun trying to suspend these economies at their most visible and most readable moment: at the moment of what I have called *libidinal education*. The material, the origin, of the literature of apprenticeship, the *Bildungsroman* brings together so many texts that relate the development of the individual, her history, the story of her soul, the story of her discovery of the world, of its pleasures and its prohibitions, its pleasures and its laws, always on the trail of the first story of all human stories, the story of *Eve and the Apple*. World literature abounds in texts of libidinal education because every writer, every artist, is brought at one moment or another to work on the genesis of his or her own artistic being, this strangeness of destiny. The *Bildungsroman* is the supreme text, written as one turns back to revisit the place where one gambles to win or lose life. The stakes are simple. A mere question of the apple: Does one eat it or not? Will one enter into contact or not with the intimate inside of the fruit?

The book begins with a primitive S-cene. Scene of the meal in which desire and prohibition coexist, opposing currents. Will I take pleasure, the hero asks himself, will I go so far as to take this pleasure and give you pleasure? And softly, the text asks itself. Come eat!

The apple, the yes, gleams, is desirable. It reigns with such an innocence that it can't help attracting famished guilt.

Will the delicious Percival of the *Quest for the Holy Grail* enjoy the marvelous meal or not? In these stories, as in childhood, the fate of the *so-called feminine economy* is at stake. I say "feminine" in connection with Percival, yes, for this economy is not the endowment solely of women. So why "feminine"? Because of the old story; because in spite of everything, ever since the Bible and ever since bibles, we have been divided up as descendants of Eve and descendants of Adam. The Book wrote this story. The Book wrote that the first person who had to deal with the question of pleasure was a woman, the woman; probably because it really was a "woman" who, in this always cultural system, underwent this test to which men and women have been subjected ever since. Every entrance to life finds itself *before the Apple*. So I resolve to qualify the relationship to pleasure, the relationship to spending, as "feminine" and "masculine" because we are born into language, and because I cannot do otherwise than to find myself preceded by words. They are there. We could change them, we could replace them with synonyms, which would become as closed, as immobile and petrifying, as the words "masculine" and "feminine," and they would lay down the law for us. And so? There is nothing to be done, except to shake them all the time, like apple trees.

"An economy said to be F.," "an economy said to be M."—why distinguish between them? Why keep words that are so entirely treacherous, dreadful, warmongering? This is where all the traps are set. I give myself poetic license; otherwise I would not dare speak. It is the poet's right to say something unusual and then to say: believe it if you want to, but believe weeping; or, as Genet does, to erase it by saying that all truths are false, that only false truths are true, and so on.

## The Scene of the *Cène*

The first fable of our first book puts our relationship to the law at stake. Enter two great puppets: the word of the Law (or the discourse of God) and the Apple. It's a struggle between the Apple and the discourse of God. In this brief scene, everything transpires before a woman. The Story begins with the Apple: at the beginning of everything, there is an apple, and this apple, when spoken of, is spoken of as a fruit-not-to. There is an apple, and straightaway there is the law. This is the first step of libidinal education: one begins by sharing in the experience of the *secret,* because the law is incomprehensible. It emits its radiations from the point of its imperceptibility. God says, "If you taste the fruit of the tree of knowledge, you will die." This is what is absolutely incomprehensible to me. For Eve, "you will die" means nothing, since she is in the paradisiacal state where there is no death. She receives the most hermetic message there is, the absolute discourse. The discourse we will find again in the story of Abraham receiving an order from God, which might also seem incomprehensible (the order to sacrifice his son, the one he loves), and which Abraham obeys absolutely, without question. This is the experience of the secret, the enigma of the apple, of this apple invested with every kind of power. We are told that knowledge could begin with the mouth, the discovery of the taste of something. Knowledge and taste go together. Yet the mystery of the stroke of the law is also staged here, absolute, verbal, invisible, negative. A symbolic *coup de force.* Its power lies in its invisibility, its nonexistence, its force of denial, its "not." And facing the law, there is the apple which is, is, is. The struggle between presence and absence, between an undesirable, unverifiable, indecisive absence, and a presence which is not only a presence: the apple is visible, is promise, is appeal—"Bring me to your lips"; it is full, it has an *inside.* What Eve will discover in her relationship to concrete reality is the inside of the apple, and this inside is good. The Fable tells us how the genesis of "femininity" goes by way of the mouth, through a certain oral pleasure, and through the nonfear of the inside.

So, in my particular fashion I read: astonishingly, our

oldest book of dreams relates to us, in its cryptic mode, that Eve is not afraid of the inside, neither of her own nor of the other's. The relationship to the interior, to penetration, to the touching of the inside, is positive. Obviously Eve is punished for it, but that is a different matter, the matter of the jealousy of God and society.

God knows what the apple must conceal, in order for death to follow the act of tasting it!

Unless it could be that the interdiction is symmetrical with the order given to Abraham, a do–not–do–that, apparently as senseless as the you–will–kill.

Unless it could be that the apple is an insignificant screen for the war between God and me.

Finally, I take the apple and bite in. Because "it's stronger than me."

A given pleasure merits a given death. This is what women think: that desire carries all. Not the hunger of Esau, but the desire to know with the lips the strange fruit and the common fruit. At the risk of losing one's life. Being ready to pay such a price is, he says, exactly what is reprehensible. It is, she says, the proof of the apple, its vital truth. Feeling pleasure means losing oneself? Losing oneself is such a joy . . .

This is where the series of "you–shall–not–enter" begins. It is not insignificant that in the beginning there is a scene of pleasure taking this form. It is a game and it is not a game.

And I rediscover it with Percival in the *Quest for the Holy Grail*. It is good to read texts that are the bearers of an unconscious completely indifferent to laws, even if the law always recaptures the wild unconscious. At first, Percival is explicitly a woman's son. He does not have a father. A boy left in his wild state, he is on the side of pleasure, of happiness. Naked. Then he is educated to become a knight, and in the process of undergoing a series of trials, he is encased in armor, phallicized, he takes up the sword. In Percival's "training," the story of Eve and the apple is once again a decisive scene. Percival, son of woman, arrives at the court of the Fisher King, a king who is deprived of the use of his legs, a king who is very hospitable and castrated. Percival is invited to a sumptuous meal, during which he takes pleasure in all the excellent foods that are served. Meanwhile a procession of servants goes by carrying splendid dishes into another room. Percival is fascinated by this merry-go-round, he is dying to ask what is going on. But only a short time before, his educator has told him, "You are wild and you have no manners, but you must learn that in life one-does-not-ask-questions." A lance passes before the unschooled one, many times. At the end of the lance, blood beads and drips. And while this is happening, the narrative intervenes: "Well, Percival, are you going to ask questions? When will you make up your mind? You are committing a terrible sin, and you will be punished." The agonized reader is caught between the narrative and the hero. And Percival, faithful schoolboy, does not ask a single question. The meal ends, the castle disappears in a flash, as in a fairy tale, and Percival meets a maiden who tells him, "Now your name is Percival"—up to this point, he has gone unnamed. So now he is punished with a *name*. Dragged by the hairs of the name out of happy anonymity and designated, denounced, set apart, to be summoned to justice. Percival has committed an unpardonable sin, the narrative puffs with indignation: he should have asked who was being served in this way, and since he did not ask, he will be punished. He is condemned for the crime (what crime?) he committed, the immediate consequences of which are catastrophic. He could have saved the Fisher King, the narrative explains to us, he could have saved the universe, but he missed the opportunity. While reading this text, the reader is seized with rage, telling herself, "It's not fair. I don't see why, and Percival doesn't see why, he is being punished for not having done something he wasn't supposed to do." "You really don't see?" whispers the narrative. We are in the world of the law, nameless, faceless, the world that has the strange "quality" of being a phantom, negative. As if the text were telling you that you are condemned to be inside the law, that you cannot do otherwise.

Proof by absurdity. This is the cruel secret, that "no one is supposed to be ignorant of the law (but in reality no one is not ignorant of it)." Fatal couple: me and the law. The abyss awaits the blind.

And at the same time, since the text is a poetic text, it takes into account the world of innocence and the world of pleasure. While the law weaves its web, Percival is extremely happy, he eats extraordinary things, enjoys himself as much as he can. And suddenly he falls, no, he is *made to fall,* into the otherworld, the world of absolute law that does not give its reasons. Although by definition indefinable, this is what the law is: pure antipleasure. What made Percival fall in this way is the fact that he is a mother's son, brought up in the forest, and still full of woman's milk. Until he is so violently "circumcized" that henceforth he will take care of his manly parts.

The relationship to pleasure and the law, and the individual's responses to this strange, antagonistic relationship, inscribe—whether we are men or women—different paths through life. It is not anatomical sex or essence that determines us in anything; it is, on the contrary, the fable from which we never escape, individual and collective history, the cultural schema, and the way the individual negotiates with these structures, with these data, adapts to them and reproduces them, or else gets around them, overcomes them, goes beyond them, gets through them—there are a thousand formulas—and connects with or never connects with a universe "without fear and without reproach." It happens that women, according to legend, have more of a chance of gaining access to pleasure. Because, virtually or actually mothers, women do after all have an experience of the inside, an experience of the capacity for other, an experience of nonnegative change brought about by the other, of positive receptivity. Isn't this true?

## Libidinal Education According to Clarice Lispector

How do we behave with the other in the major experiences of life—experiences of separation, experiences, in love, of possession and dispossession, of incorporation and nonincorporation; experiences of mourning by allusion, of real mourning, all the experiences governed by economies, variable structures? How do we lose? How do we keep? Do we remember? Do we forget? Do we take? Do we receive?

The work of Clarice Lispector stages all the possible positions of the pleasuring subject in his or her relation to acts of appropriation. Scenes of use and abuse of ownership. And she has done this through the most subtle and delicate details. The text struggles endlessly against the movement of appropriation, which, even in its most innocent guises, is fatally destructive. Isn't pity destructive? Badly thought-out love is destructive; ill-measured understanding is anni-hilating. We think we are holding out a hand? We hit. The work of Clarice Lispector is an immense *book of respect. Book of the right distance.* And, as she tells us in numerous narratives, one can attain this proper distance only through a relentless process of de-selfing, de-egoization. The enemy, so far as she is concerned, is the blind, greedy ego. In *The Hour of the Star* she says, for example, "The action of this story will have as a result my transfiguration into the other and eventually my materialization into object. Yes, and maybe I will reach the sweet flute into which I will curl up as a tender creeper."[7]

We might say this is only a metaphor; but it is the dream of every author to arrive at such a transfiguration of the self, such a remove that I become vine. A way of remembering that my self is only one of the elements of the immense material universe, one of the elements haunted by the imaginary. "Although I want bells to peal in order to animate me, while I guess reality. And I want angels to be flitting around my hot head like transparent wasps, because this head wants finally to transform itself into an object-thing, that's easier."[8]

There is also the constant reminder of what we know, in the form of a cliché: that we are dust. That we are atoms. And if we did not forget that we were atoms, we would live and love differently. More humbly. More expansively. Loving the "you ares" of the world, equal to equal. Without design. "And here I am dedicating this thing here to old Schumann and his sweet Clara, who today are bones, poor us. I dedicate myself to the color red, very scarlet, like this blood of mine which is that of a man in his prime, and hence I dedicate myself to my own blood . . . [and] to all

those who have reached unexpected zones in me in a terrifying way, all our prophets of the present time who have
predicted me to myself to such a degree that in this very
instant I explode into: I."[9]

The feature that comes through immediately in this dedication (apart from the fact that "the truth" is between-
parentheses-Clarice-Lispector) is the "I dedicate *myself*." I
read first "I am dedicating *this thing* here to old Schumann."
Is this thing the book? No. The following sentence dedi-
cates "myself": "*I dedicate myself to the color red, very scarlet
like this blood of mine.*" In other words, "this thing" that is
the book is "I." We are already on the road of metamorphoses: "I dedicate myself above all to the gnomes, dwarfs,
sylphs, and nymphs who inhabit my life." Let's continue
the length of this crucial and mutinous road of the body.

This I who is you, for I can't bear being simply me, I need others
to keep me standing, and giddy as I am, I obliquely, finally, what
is there to do except meditate in order to fall into this full void
which one only reaches through meditation. Meditation needs
no results. Meditation can have itself as an end, I meditate without
words and on nothingness. What tangles my life is writing.

Yes, and not to forget that the structure of the atom is not
visible. But we're informed. I'm aware of many things I haven't
seen, and you too. One cannot give a proof of the existence of
what is truer, the trick is to believe. To believe weeping.[10]

And to think that we spend precious months of our
existence trying to give "proofs," falling into the trap of
critical interpellation, allowing ourselves to be led before
the critical tribunal, where we are told: "Give us proof,
explain to us what 'feminine writing' or 'sexual difference'
is." I should retort: "A flute for proof—I am alive." A

sweetly tangled flute . . . I am not serene enough, except when I write. And when I write, I tell myself: "This is not enough, we need to do something else. *Explain*." Explain the inexplicable. However, it is true that what is most true goes like this: either you know without knowing, and this unknowing knowledge is a flash of joy the other shares with you, or else there is nothing. You'll never convert someone who is not already converted. You'll never touch a heart planted on another planet.

## Knowing How to Have What One Has

Clarice's texts tell the stories of illuminations, "facts," as she says, the moments, the nows of life that play out abrupt dramas. Not theatrical tragedies, but dramas that make up the living of life. In this way one can name what is in convulsion, seeking to manifest itself, realize itself, hatch into thought. A series of texts work on the question of having, of knowing how to have what one has. This is one of the most difficult things in the world. Poor humans that we are, no sooner do we have than we no longer have. We are often like the fisherman's wife in the tale, unhappily prey to the demon of having, of always-having-more: she never has any of what she has; as soon as she has, she wants the next degree, and so on all the way to infinity, which returns her to zero. Having what we have is the key to happiness. We have, we have a great deal, but because we have, and as soon as we have, we no longer know that we have.

What can we do to have what we have? There is a secret to it: it is *Clandestine Felicity*[11]—a story about childhood, a little prophetic book just a few pages long. There are two

little girls. One is little Clarice. The other is a little red-
headed friend whose father owns a bookstore, and so she is
surely in paradise. She has the father and the books. But
by chance (life is like this), the redheaded girl from the
bookstore is a little pest. A bad witch. She tells Clarice she
is going to lend her an enormous and extraordinary book.
She keeps her walking, running, for weeks telling her,
"Come over to my house and I'll give it to you." Clarice
goes across town in a state of absolute happiness. Under
the footsteps of the enchanted one, the world turns to sea.
The entire world is pleasuring. She gets there, the horrid
little redhead opens the door and tells her each time, "I
don't have it, come back next week." Clarice plunges down
from the heaven of hope, from hope-heaven. And gets back
up. Collapse, flight, the one following the other in a pattern
of rebirths. Without fail, Clarice returns to the door, until
the day when the mother of the horrid little girl happens to
be on the scene and discovers the mechanism of hate that
has been put into operation. The mother is devastated by
the discovery of her daughter's wickedness, but, mother of
all the little girls in the world, she immediately makes
amends. The book must be lent! And furthermore, Clarice
adds, the mother says, "You may keep it as long as you
wish." The mother gives the desiring one the endlessness
of the book. Misfortune of joy! From the moment Clarice
can dispose of this book endlessly, what will become of the
race across town, the desire, the twisted and tortured joy?
Will everything escape her because she has everything,
forever? But there is a limit: the book has not been given to
her, it has been given to her to keep for as long as she wants.
And this is the moral of the story: it is yours for as long as
you have the strength to want it. So Clarice invents the

marvelous, magical means, the positive sorcery, the art of remaining on the brink, to make this "as long as" interminable. She *has* the book; what must she do to "have" it? A present must be invented that will not stop presenting itself. This is where she begins to enjoy what she has and not what she desires. By a sort of fabulous intuition she stages the having, makes it palpitate, move slightly, vibrate, she does not consume it, she does not devour it: first making a sandwich, coming and going between the kitchen and the book, the bread sandwich and the textual sandwich that she does not devour, sitting down in a hammock with her book on her knees, she literally rocks it, and she does not read, does not read, not yet—and then she goes off again. And she finds all the most profound, delicate, subtle ruses to continue having what she has eternally, to not lose having, to be pregnant with having, is—guesses—the text, already, in the child, in the woman, already the lover who savors the wait and the promise, happy already to have something to enjoy, happy that there is, in the world, the to-be-enjoyed, the world that is the book of promises. And this happiness that is also the portent of happiness she calls "clandestine felicity."

Yes, felicity can only be clandestine, will always be clandestine, happiness is its own secret, one can really have only if one knows how to have in a way that does not destroy, does not possess.

The secret: remembering at every instant the grace of having.

Keeping in this having the breathless lightness of hoping to have. Barely having after not having had. Always keeping in oneself the emotion of almost not having had. Having is always a miracle.

While having, rediscovering endlessly the surprise of receiving. The illumination of arrival.

These lessons of knowing slip out into our laps from the texts of Clarice Lispector, lessons of knowing, but of knowing how to live, not of scholarly knowledge. One of the first lessons about living is the one that consists of *knowing how not to know,* which does not mean not knowing, but knowing how to not know, knowing how to avoid getting closed in by knowledge, knowing more and less than what one knows, knowing how not to understand, while never being on the side of ignorance. It is not a question of not having understood anything, but of not letting oneself get locked into comprehension. Each time that we come to know something, in reality it is a step. Then we have to strike out for the un-known, to make our way along in the dark, with an "apple in our hand" like a candle.[12] To see the world with the fingers: isn't this actually writing *par excellence*?

To find the apple by feeling one's way along in the dark —this is the condition of discovery, this is the condition of love. As Clarice says in *The Foreign Legion:* "Then—then, because I do not know how to do anything and because I cannot remember anything and because it is night—then I would stretch out my hand and save a child."[13] So I translate: I can save a child only on two conditions (one is merely the condition of the other): on condition of not preceding the child, on condition of not knowing any more than he or she does; of not having the massive old heavy memory that would crush the young budding memory of the child. It is only from the dark of my night that I can hold out my hand and tenderly provide help.

*The Foreign Legion?* A pitiless tale that concerns the adult

Clarice and a little girl who lives in her building and whose name is Ofelia. This little girl is in the habit of forcefully inviting herself into Clarice's apartment. She is a little premature woman, not by virtue but by default, by aggression, naïve violence, in absolute mastery; she is imperious, authoritative, and she instructs Clarice, "You should not have bought this, you should not have done that," scolds, master little girl, until one day the little girl becomes a little girl again under the influence of a gift. One day Ofelia hears a cheeping sound in the kitchen. The cheeping of a tiny baby chick. For the first time, something precedes her; she is caught off guard. Clarice sees a terrible drama in Ofelia's eyes: she has been pierced for the first time by the torturing arrow of desire. She struggles as if in a death agony against the pain of this desire, she does not want to enter this wounded world, this world of love, and be at the mercy of the other. It is with her reluctant body that she discovers how desire can present an opening to the other, a possibility of being wounded, being altered. Finally she succumbs, she cannot help seeing the desire mounting in her, but she does not want to show this to Clarice. There follows a series of maneuvers on the part of the little girl. How to reveal the wound, reveal the desire, without demeaning herself. Then there is a wonderful scene composed entirely of the silences and the ruses of love. Clarice approaches imperceptibly: How can she give the chick to the little girl who, she can see, will die if she does not have it? Even though she cannot give it to her, because the little girl, erect, stiff with refusal, her heartstrings taut, would find herself in the position of someone to whom one has given an intolerable gift, the kind that engenders debt. All of the simplest, the most elementary, the most terrible mechanisms of gift and debt, of exchange and gratitude, are put into operation. If the little girł has to say thank you, she will not have anything. Thus, the only means of giving her the chick is to let her take it: Clarice, in the position of the symbolic mother, must efface herself, must retire in such a way that the child may benefit from the gift as if it were given by God, by no one, and thus be free of all feelings of debt. Clarice becomes silence. Nonexistent. The little girl finally goes to the kitchen alone. The text notes an immense silence, the little girl comes back, Clarice rushes into the kitchen and finds the chick dead. In the kitchen the drama of our daily mourning has played itself out, we who are so often the victims of debt. The inevitability of this scene: Clarice has given the baby chick to the little girl as best she can, no more, no less. But the state of the little girl is such that she can possess the chick only by losing it the moment she has it. The chick is too much for her. And yet she has had it as much but also as little as she was able. And yet Clarice let her take it as much as she was able to, and thus to the point of total loss.

## The Benediction of Need

It is in *The Passion According to G.H.* that all the mysteries of loving—at once so subtle and so paradoxical that loving sometimes resembles not-loving in the same way that one tear resembles another—are explained page by page, with a mad patience.

The Passion, hymn to need. Celebration of life as a fatality of the hunger and thirst for you.

"I need your hand now, not so I won't be afraid but so you won't. I know belief in all this will, in the beginning, be a great solitude for you. But the moment will arrive

when you will give me your hand, no longer in solitude,
but as I do now: in love. Just like me, you won't be afraid
to add yourself to God's extreme energetic sweetness. Solitude is simply having human destiny. And solitude is not
needing."

Listen to it carefully. This is really the most beautiful, the
noblest definition of a certain economy that I will let myself
go so far as to call "feminine": "Not needing leaves a [man]
alone, all alone. Oh, needing doesn't isolate a person, things
need things . . . " Man? But saying "man" is also a subtle
humility for a thinking woman. "Oh, my love, don't be
afraid of that lacking: it is our greater destiny. Love is so
much more fateful than I thought, love is as ingrained as is
lack itself, and we are guaranteed by necessity that it is
continually renewed. Love is now, is always."[14]

What *she,* woman, is establishing here in this hymn-to-
want is the economy of positive lack: lack, above all, let us
not lack. Lack is also wealth: "Love is so much more
fateful . . . Love is now, love is always." "And miracles too
can be sought and had, for continuity has interstices that
don't make it discontinuous, the miracle is the note that lies
between two musical notes, the note that lies between the
number one and the number two. It's just a question of
seeking and having."[15]

It is enough just to need and we have. It is enough not to
be afraid of needing and we have. It is enough not to
proceed like little Ofelia, who was afraid of needing and
who leaped with a bound into the scene of castration.

"Love is now." It is there. It precedes us as the poem
precedes the poet. "All that is missing is the *coup de grâce*—
which is called passion."[16] This is *the economy of recognition.*
All we need to do is live, and we have. Another way to say
this: hunger is faith.

But Kafka, at the same extremity of life, says this: *"Man kann doch nicht nicht-leben"* ("One cannot not-live, after all").[17] The economy of double powerlessness.

At the end of life, and before death, Kafka and Clarice Lispector ask themselves how to accomplish the truth of our human being.

Clarice is on the side of the yes: "It is enough to live and this in itself becomes a great goodness." Anyone who accepts living is good, anyone who is thankful for living is good and does good: Is this sainthood, according to Clarice Lispector? A modest kind of sainthood. From the other shore of living, Kafka says, *"Dass es uns an Glauben fehle, kann man nicht sagen"* ("It cannot be said that we are lacking in faith").

Here one is in negative discourse. Everything is there— faith, lack, need, life; but everything is caught up in the not. Resignation to existence, not exaltation of it. *"Dass es uns an Glauben fehle, kann man nicht sagen. Allein die einfache Tatsache unseres Lebens ist in ihrem Glaubenswert garnicht auszuschöpfen."* ("It cannot be said that we are lacking in faith. Even the simple fact of our life is of a faith-value that can never be exhausted.") And then he adds: *"Hier wäre ein Glaubenswert?"* ("You suggest there is some faith value in this?") And replies, because he is a divided being: *"Man kann doch nicht nicht-leben."* *"Eben in diesem, 'kann doch nicht' steckt die wahnsinnige Kraft des Glaubens; in dieser Verneinung bekommt sie Gestalt."* ("One cannot not-live, after all." "It is precisely in this 'cannot, after all' that the mad strength of faith lies; it is in this negation that it takes on form.")[18]

One cannot not: this is the opposite in the same field of meditation, of Clarice's faith: to come to think that solitude means not to need, that to need is already to break with solitude, is the greatest lesson in humility, where thirst is itself what slakes thirst, because being thirsty is already letting oneself experience, drink, open the door.

Needing is a spiritual offering of one's hand to the other, and offering one's hand is not a demand; it is a greeting to the world, a giving place. Needing is mute trust. Is strength.

## The World of Gentle Hands

Rare indeed are texts like Clarice's: without denying that we all have to cope with solitude, these texts extend their hand to us and help us attain the world of mansuetude. I am taking the word "mansuetude" literally: it is *the custom of offering one's hand.*

"Tanta Mansidão," or "Such Gentleness," evokes in mild ecstasy the scene of the primitive scenes, the scene of meeting without consuming. Two economies are contrasted almost explicitly in a delicate epiphany: the economy of consolation and the economy of acceptance.

| *"Tanta Mansidão"* | *"Such Gentleness"* |
|---|---|
| *Vou então à janela, está chovendo muito. Por hábito estou procurando na chuva o que em outro momento me serviria de consolo. Mas não tenho dor a consolar.* | I go, then, to the window; it is raining heavily. By habit I search in the rain for what at another time would serve to console me. But I have no grief to console.[19] |

Previously, Clarice tells us, "I" was "organized" in such a way as to console my anguish. Organization, anguish, consolation are the elements of a classic structure of defense: our daily way of feeling ourselves to be besieged by existence, and of responding, parrying. We respond to anguish with consolation, in an unnamed struggle. Pain is ceaselessly exchanged for joy. But now, before the window, another universe starts: there, without struggle, without "against," "I" experience a simple joy, not conquered but admitted. And this joy is like the hand of a blessing. Nothing arrives. The blessing gives. It falls with regularity.

*Apenas isso: chove e estou vendo a chuva. Que simplicidade. Nunca pensei que o mundo e eu chegássemos a esse ponto de trigo. A chuva cai não porque está precisando de mim, e eu olho a chuva não porque preciso dela. Mas nós estamos tão juntas como a água da chuva está ligada à chuva. E eu não estou agradecendo nada. Não tivesse eu, logo depois de nascer, tomado involuntária e forçadamente o caminho que tomei—e teria sido sempre o que realmente estou sendo: uma camponesa que está num campo onde chove. Nem sequer agradecendo ao Deus ou à natureza. A chuva também não agradece nada. Não sou uma coisa que agradece ter se transformado em outra. Sou uma mulher, sou uma pessoa, sou uma atenção, sou um corpo olhando pela janela. Assim como a chuva não é grata por não ser uma pedra. Ela é uma chuva. Talvez seja isso ao que se poderia chamar de estar vivo. Não mais que isto, mas isto: vivo. E apenas vivo de uma alegria mansa.*

Only this: it rains, and I watch the rain. What simplicity. I never thought that the world and I would reach this point [of wheat]. The rain falls, not because it needs me, and I look at the rain, not because I need it. But we are as united as the water of the rain is to the rain. And I'm not giving thanks for anything. If shortly after birth I hadn't taken, involuntarily, by compulsion, the road I took—I would always have been what in fact I really am: a country girl in a field where it is raining. Not even thanking God or nature. The rain, too, expresses no gratitude. I am not a thing that is thankful for having been transformed into something else. I am a woman, I am a person, I am an attention. I am a body looking out through the window. Just as the rain is not grateful for not being a stone. It is rain. Perhaps it is this that might be called being alive. No more than this, but this: alive. And alive just through gentle gladness.[20]

There is the world and the self: everything. "I go, then, to the window; it is raining hard." It is the meeting of two equivalents. Thus, I go to the window: and similarly it is raining hard. Not Genet's equivalents, for whom all beings are equivalent to one another by the wound of castration. She and the rain—these are the subjects of the moment. While I go, it is raining. The rain and I—two equally important subjects, two agents of life . . .

The encounter is called this marvelous thing: "this point of wheat." There where she and the rain are simultaneously, there is wheat. And then this affirmation with its implacable justice: "I am not a thing that is thankful for having been transformed into something else." No thanks, no pity, no acknowledgment, no debt, but being, being, with insistence—without commentary. A pure "here I am." "I am a woman, I am a person, I am an attention. I am a body looking out through the window. Just as the rain is not grateful for not being a stone."

She is a rainfall. She is not a not being something other than what she is. Raining rain. Separation of positive and negative. I am not she-who-is-not; I am, am, am. Perhaps that is what one could call living: the plain miracle of being. Wheat: fertility of the being as being at the window of the world.

Certainly not everyone can be situated there where Clarice situates herself: beyond anguish, beyond mourning, in the magnificent acceptance of being she who encounters simply the rain, and perhaps simply the earth. One needs to be very strong and very humble to be able to say "I am a woman," continuing with "I am a person, I am an attention." Not "I am a woman," period. But "I am a body looking out through the window." Anyone who can say, "I am a body looking out through a window," can say, "(I) am a woman": without "I," without personal pronoun, woman is pure "am," activity of being that does not lead back to the self, woman is the one who "is" *woman and, woman-making-her-way-in-the-world-taking-heed.*

Heed. Need. Woman does not stop at woman, doesn't stop, flows, writes herself in parataxes of liquid light, tears, and her style is *Agua Viva,* the stream of life.[21]

## This "I" Who Is You

Who are you who are so strangely me?

In numerous texts by Clarice Lispector, the most extreme approach, the greatest tension, is situated between the human subject and the nonhuman subject. The partner, the other, the one with whom it becomes a question of establishing a love relationship at the end of a very long quest, is the rat in "Vengeance and Painful Reconciliation."[22] In the text called "Mineirinho,"[23] the other is a sort of human rat, a delinquent, a bandit, who is killed like a animal, and with whom Clarice has the greatest difficulty establishing the point of wheat. Or else it is the cockroach in *The Passion According to G.H.* This woman, G.H., who does not have a name, of whom only the barest initials remain, travels a long way back to the immemorial cockroach. She travels a hundred thousand years in a room (this cockroach is the great Brazilian cockroach; and *barata* is feminine in Brazilian), and she (who?) will come to the end of this painstaking journey—just as the *barata* has come, immobile, from a hundred thousand years back. Not a single step in this travel can be skipped, or all would be lost—the meaning, the meeting, the revelation; one must not skip a stage in this step-by-step process, where the steps are not only human steps, but also cockroach steps, destination Woman. It is therefore on all fours that she makes her way to the cock-roach. To the famous immense scene which must not be misunderstood: the scene of "tasting the cockroach."

It happens, in a certain chapter of this clandestine Bible, that G.H. thinks she has at last reached the point of matur-ation where she will be able to love the right way, to make space for the other, to make the supreme gesture with regard to the cockroach. Having inadvertently trapped the cockroach in the cupboard door, and the cockroach having let out a little of its juice, of its matter (but cockroaches are immortal beings, they have existed for millions of years), she brings to her mouth this white issue of the *barata,* and then a violent incident takes place: she (G.H.) disap-pears, she vomits with disgust, she faints, vomits herself up. And the marvelous thing about this story: she imme-diately realizes, passing through the portal of error, that she was mistaken. Her mistake was that she did not give up the space to the other, and that, in the immoderation of love, she told herself, "I am going to overcome my disgust, and I am going to go as far as the gesture of supreme commu-nion. I am going to kiss the leper." But the kiss of the leper transformed into metaphor lost its truth.

Communing with the material of the *barata* is a kind of grandiloquence. Too much desire and too much knowledge taint the act and cause G.H. *to fall* into heroism. Eating the *barata* is not a proof of sainthood; it is an idea. This is the mistake. Zealous, but not wise, G.H. makes the gesture, which she does not analyze at the time, of incorporation. Immediately castigated by a flash of truth, she brings up the cockroach, and the step-by-step, page-by-page, insect-like approach starts up again all the way to the ultimate revelation. The text teaches us that the most difficult thing to do is to arrive at the most extreme proximity while guarding against the trap of projection, of identification. The other must remain absolutely strange within the greatest possible proximity.

And must be respected according to its species, without violence, with the neutrality of the Creator, the equal and undemonstrative love with regard to each being. (What was the voice of God like *speaking* in Genesis? Its flat and all-powerful music?)

In *The Passion,* the subject with whom Clarice does her apprenticeship of ultimate impassion, the love partner, is sufficiently strange to make the asceticism of this troubling work more obvious to us than if the other were an ordinary human subject. Love your fellow being as if he were your stranger. Love her whom you do not understand. Love me, love your *barata,* you my love, my *barata.* Yes, Clarice's ultimate project is to make the other human subject appear equal—and this is positive—to the roach. Each to her own species.

This is where I find myself back at *The Hour of the Star,* where Macabea (this is the name that the scarcely-a-woman will bear very late in the text, the name she comes into and which prophesies) is in the place of the cockroach. Macabea is a talking cockroach, and as ancient, as primitive as the cockroach. And, like it, is destined to be . . . crushed.

And the strange "acquaintance" is made with the assistance of, to the accompaniment of, music, by its grace: "And above all I dedicate myself to the eves of today and to today, to the transparent veil of Debussy, to Marlos Nobre, etc., to the dodecaphonics, to the bitter cries of the electronics—to all those who have reached unexpected zones in me in a terrifying way, all our prophets of the present time." Poets, musicians, announcers of what is, of the present we too often miss, we who do not know how to be the contemporaries of our own nows. "Who have predicted me to myself to such a degree that in this very instant I explode into: I."

Those who help us explode into "I" are perhaps those who, by paths that are not the paths of discourse but paths of the voice, reach and awaken in us the "unexpected zones." Those who are the thieves of fire, the thieves of music. They live only in "The Author's Dedication," because the author, he, has culture.

But in the text, these giants, "our prophets of the present time," do not exist. Debussy, Schoenberg or Prokofiev, each of whom touches "the author" in a different point of the body, do not exist for the lowly characters who are the inhabitants of the book. Once we have entered the poverty of the text through another door (the door of dust), what remains of these great lords of music is what punctuates the text from time to time in a painful way for us: a street violonist, for example, whose sawing we hear interrupted now and then in the text; and there is the whole range of protest. On the first page we have the jangling of the most elementary music: "The toothache that runs through this story has given me an intense twinge right in the mouth. So I sing high and sharp a strident, syncopated melody—it is my own pain, I who carry the world, and there is a lack of happiness."[24]

Let me come back to the music. At first I was touched by certain characters who vibrate vividly in *Jerusalem Delivered*. I was struck by the interplay of the categories of "the faithful" and "the unfaithful." The faithful and the unfaithful constantly interchange, as "men" and "women" do in the domain of sexual difference. There are two couples of lovers. One of them is the classical couple, Rinaldo and Armida, in which a banal story of seduction is played out between a *femme fatale* and a castrated man. And there is the other couple, Tancredi and Clorinda, who remain outside the scene of seduction, in a state of admiration—a value we never talk about enough, akin to respect. Tancredi and Clorinda, to all appearances two knights (but really two women). There is an imaginary universe in literature where one meets "the armed woman." Did the Amazon exist? She may have been fantasy, or historical reality—I know nothing about it. In the most ancient of epic poems, in the most ancient stories, women go forth to meet men as equals in the exercise of power and war, and this always turns into love. I would like to know who "in truth" the "author" of this story is. Unless it could be that this story is itself the author of the author, the fantastic genitrix of Homer, Kleist, Tasso . . . ? Is it Achilles who tries to cross over to the side of femininity, is it Penthesilea who would like to reconcile the obligation of being a man with the need to be a woman, or is it Achilles? Who was Kleist, this "man" so exuberant with women (in truth)? And Tasso, haunted by Clorinda? Clorinda, the best warrior of the infidel army, is a woman, and the most faithful of women. What is beautiful about the story of *Jerusalem Delivered* is that Tancredi pursues Clorinda, equal pursues equal, the strongest pursues the strongest, the most beautiful pursues the most beautiful. Until Clorinda accidentally loses her helmet, and Tancredi, in a dazzling scene, sees that the being who has attracted him across fields and through songs has long hair. And so the drama that promises them and forbids them to each other is set ablaze. Tancredi adores Clorinda, but everything separates them. For they are subjects of the fatality that governs all great epics, all great dreams conveying the lament of glorious femininity. To realize their desire in this world, they would both have to be unfaithful to their being. Of course, it is to be faithful to their secret being that each exerts her force and makes himself desirable to whoever has guessed it. Clorinda, to have the right to fight, must pretend to be a man in order to spare men the scandal of a woman as good as they are. The wedding could occur only in an "unexpected zone."[25]

And as happens to Percival in the *Quest for the Holy Grail,* the law intervenes to say, "Be careful; we are in the world of the law, even if you think you are free of it." Reality falls like a counter-revolution on these epics, where the nostalgia for a happy love between two equal masculine and feminine forces shimmers. If we were going to allow humanity to take pleasure, would we dream it, fear it? No; so we can be sure that Tancredi and Clorinda will come to grief, *because* they love each other as equals, with equal strength, equal loyalty. History will not tolerate Paradise on earth; one of them has to die. The vanquished author wakes up, dead. And in this last terrible and accidental struggle, Tancredi kills Clorinda, because he has not recognized her in a different helmet. They rejoin each other in death, because there, at least, history does not follow.

I follow in the footsteps of Tancredi and I come to Rossini's *Tancredi.* Here is a story in which the musician has heard the most profound reality with the ear of Desire. What he has heard is the incomprehensible truth of this particular love. The pursuit starts up again, but this time in the feminine. For without any explanation, with that marvelous right of musicians that I envy, Tancredi, the champion of the faithful, is sung by a woman, and no one in the theater comes to demand an explanation. Tearful, one listens and one believes. It is in the world of music that a certain strength full of gentleness is assigned, without any ulterior motives and without any premeditation, to a hero with a woman soul, in a woman body. Rossini's Tancredi doesn't turn around to ask, "Am I a man or a woman?" It is also true that Clorinda can be loved only by a Tancreda. Such a love makes a person into a woman. (The man) who can die of love is a woman. Dying, which is to say loving his fellow creature above himself. In *Jerusalem Delivered,* there are a man and a woman who wear armor. Yes, armor bothers me, this false manly skin. But how are these disguises to be gotten rid of? Let's slip out "by the back door." If you hear the Tancreda of Rossini, these questions no longer exist. Deep down, they are two women. Still, one of them is just as much a man, but a man by woman truth. These are mysteries that we sometimes live out in our daily lives, in the secret zones where one senses wordlessly like the dreamer stretched out on the bank of his dream.

How poignant the dream of the author who wants to love a woman from extremely close up, to love the essence in her, to pleasure in the femininity in her, to read the book of flesh that does not lie, does not hold back, has not started to tell a story. A dream that a woman author can have more easily than a man author.

Yes, but it can happen that an author, a woman, comes too close to a woman to get to make her acquaintance, in the sense of discovering her still unknown. And thus, through familiarity, she misses her. What to do? A trip around the world to make an entrance from the other side, this time as a stranger.

Enter Rodrigo S.M., in order more thoroughly not to know and then to know Macabea.

If in *The Hour of the Star* there is a metamorphosis, it is in the movement of recognition of the unhoped-for other. And this movement is perhaps expressed in a confidence which "the author (in truth Clarice Lispector)" makes when he (she) says, at the highest point of the inscription of the virtuality of the other: "(When I think that I might have been born her . . . )."[26]

The author is talking about Macabea, who does not yet have a name: "But she had pleasures. On icy nights, shivering under the canvas sheet, she would read by candlelight the ads she had cut out of old newspapers lying around the office. Because she collected ads, and pasted them in an album."

These are pleasures that we no longer have. We are people living after-the-lobster. But before-the-lobster, one has the greatest pleasures in the world. Everything that is marvelous, not yet, and forever. For example, this vast world of "ads," the world of promises. By collecting advertisements, "she" brings about the re-creation of the Promised Land. And here she is before a colorful version of the first Apple.

There was an ad, the most precious, which showed, in color, the open jar of a cream for the skin of women who were simply not her. Performing the fatal tic she had caught, of blinking, she would start imagining with gusto. The cream was so appetizing that, if she had had money to buy it, she wouldn't be stupid. For the skin, nothing! She would eat it, that's it, spoonfuls out of the jar. Because she lacked fat, and her body was as dry as a half-empty paperbag of crumbled toast. With time, she had become mere living matter in its primary form. Maybe she was like that in order to defend herself from the great temptation of being unhappy, once and for all, and of pitying herself. When I think that I might have been born her—and why not? I shiver. It seems to me that not to be her is a cowardly escape. I feel guilty, as I have said in one of the titles for this book.[27]

The "most precious" ad is the one that puts in question all the poverty in femininity, as well as all the possible richness in femininity. In this paragraph, we, character, reader, author, circulate between "I am not her," and "I could be her," as we advance along the most powerful path of meditation that we can take in thinking of the other. In general, when we think of the other, the stranger, without the narcissistic investment of love, it is in terms of negative nonidentification, of exclusion. Here, in the autobiography-by-proxy of Macabea, "I" is also the wom(e)n that I am not, the first person is also the third, and the third *is* the first.

One theme of the narrative is recognition of the difference of the other, but accompanied continually, for the subject, by the possibility of being the other. Thus, the women "simply were not her," and if she had the jar— marvelous thing—she would do with it what those who live after-the-lobster would never think of doing. She would eat it. For she, still without a name but not without imagination, is at the most rudimentary level of cream, of the beginning of cream, at the most elementary level of food. Before the jar. She is made of "crumbled toast." Her ovaries: "little dry mushrooms."[28] That is how she sees herself, without pathos. The "great temptation of being unhappy once and for all, and of pitying herself" would deprive her of the joy of being alive.

But (she) who in order to tell us Macabea's imaginary

delicacies had to go as far as Rodrigo S.M., voyager from
another sex, is one of those who put cream on their skin.
Because, in order to guess Macabea more accurately, Clarice Lispector must also distance herself from herself and be
able to become one of them, the rich women (whom Macabea is not), without self-pity or pity for others. Reading
this narrative I sometimes almost forgot her, I did forget
her. Later I remembered. And for one second, through
Macabea's eyes, I saw Clarice Lispector heavily made-up,
coming out of the salon where having her hair done had
cost a month's worth of sausage sandwiches. Or was it
myself I saw? A political text, then? Subreptitiously. If
there is a politics of spirituality. In the implacably realist
*and* spiritual world of Clarice Lispector, poverty and wealth
are first of all conditions of the soul, paradoxical figures of
passion.

Treatise of joy: it is enough to live, this is the miracle.
Who can say "in truth," who can really live this ascetic joy?
Macabea. (No, I don't want to hear what resounds in that
name.)

So our Macabea, in her infinite poverty, preserves the "it
is enough to live" of *The Passion According to G.H.* What
she has is simply living. Not the eating and drinking that
she is almost without. This poverty is her wealth. It is what
we do not have, we who have lost the paradise of before-
the-lobster. "(When I consider that I might been born
her . . . )," sighs the author in the masculine, crouched in
his parenthesis like a prompter: "I" who is you, and who
thus could be her, but who happily and unhappily is not
her. This is the opposite of the parenthesis of the dedication
that says: "Dedication by the Author (in truth Clarice Lispector)." Here in the parenthesis, "(When I think that I

might have been born her—and why not?—I shiver)," the climax of the development inaugurated in "(in truth Clarice Lispector)" is inscribed. All the chances are in the parentheses. It is a matter of chances of chances, the chance of birth, the moment when matter precipitates itself into form, and gives a Macabea or an author or Clarice or you. This chance is in the parenthesis. "Why not?"—this is Clarice's ethical question. I was born Clarice, but by chance. Chance: she was born in the Ukraine and she writes in Brazilian. She could as well have been a pygmy, and why not? We always identify with our chances, our accidents, we the superior beings of after-the-lobster.

But this identification is narcissistic and impoverishing. We are much more than what our own name authorizes us and obligates us to believe we are.

We are *possible*. Anyone. We need only avoid closing up the parentheses in which our "why-nots" live. Thus, I am a person who begins a long time before me, with the first molecules, and who continues after me and all around me. However, and by chance, I am a woman, and I belong to the human race. Oh yes, I am human and also a woman.

And at the same time, it is the confession of terror: if I the author, "Rodrigo S.M.," had been born Macabea. "(The fact that I am not her strikes me as being a cowardly escape. I feel remorse, as I explained in one of my titles for this book.)" And yet the text will have been an immense endeavor to know at least one life of Macabea.

At least one hour of this life.

At least one breath of this life.

Because in the final hour, everyone is equally poor, equally rich, equally subject to the star.

A difficult book written with courage without pity, neither for me nor for you, by a dying woman. So poor in life and yet at every second fabulously rich.

When Clarice goes by way of Macabea, after a series of metamorphoses, when she returns to the matter, reappears as a masculine author, and so on, this is the moment when she will soon really cease to be a person called Clarice Lispector. The moment of this metamorphosis is so brief —*The Hour of the Star* is a very short book—that you can read it in an hour, this story of the life of Clarice Lispector, the last. It is perhaps, in effect, in her last hour that "the author (in truth Clarice Lispector)" will have succeeded in being born Macabea. Macabea, the name of Clarice Lispector become no one, and whose live elements are there, invisible, in the air we breathe.

The author of *The Hour of the Star* is a woman of mortal delicacy.

The author of *The Hour of the Star* is born out of the necessity of this text, and he dies with the text. He is the work of his work. He is the child, the father, and (in truth the mother).

He has been brought into the world with the mission of loving, in the best way possible, the scarcely-a-woman Macabea. Loving her entirely and in detail, she whom no one other than No One has known how to love.

And with the mission of loving her sparse hair and her sex of nevertheless-a-woman. This is the delicate task that Clarice Lispector has entrusted to the author she created expressly for Macabea, for perhaps a certain woman (in truth Clarice Lispector) would not have dared to contemplate a woman's sex?

And perhaps the modest Macabea would have been much

more frightened by the gaze of a lady than by that of a man, perhaps a doctor. So, out of love, Clarice withdraws, and delegates Rodrigo S.M. to Macabea.

And is it not just that characters should have a right to the author who is *best placed* to understand them and give them life?

Obviously this remark holds true only for books in which there is a question of *loving,* of respecting.

And respect must begin *before* the book.

How far it is from a star to a self, O what inconceivable proximity between one species and another, between an adult and a child, between an author and a character what secret proximity.

Everything is far away, not everything resides only in distance, everything is less distant than we think, in the end everything touches, touches us.

Just as Macabea got into Clarice's eye, like a speck of dust, just as she made her weep tears of believing, I am touched by Clarice's voice.

The step of her slow, heavy phrases weighs on my heart, she treads with short heavy phrases, thoughtfully.

Sometimes one has to go very far.
Sometimes the right distance is extreme remoteness.
Sometimes it is in extreme proximity that she breathes.

# Coming to Reading Hélène Cixous

## by Deborah Jenson

In Hélène Cixous's 1976 essay "Coming to Writing," a remarkable "capitalist-realist superuncle," an "Anti-other in papaperson," rehashes the sober facts of the narrator's failure to allow herself to be captured within a recognizable literary tradition: "We think you're here," he says, "and you're there. One day we tell ourselves: this time we've got her, it's her for sure. This woman is in the bag. And we haven't finished pulling the purse strings when we see you come in through another door." Today, in the 1990s, Cixous's writing has become a part of recognizable literary history. But her texts still manage to lead the expectant reader on a chase—and not only the capitalist-realist super-reader, but the other reader, the one who is willing to accompany the narrator on her path to writing. "Am *I* here?" the reader might ask, "or am *I* there? And what is in that bag?" Pursuing the elusive author not only in her trapdoor escapes into the new, but in her wanderings back into the fairytale forest of the familiar, the reader strays deeper and deeper into the question of how to read one's way to writing . . .

*"Coming to Writing" and Other Essays* groups together much of Cixous's work in the essay form from 1976 to 1989. The collection's coherence rests less in any one thematic than in the development of Cixous's readings of artistic sources—literature, opera, and painting—over the years, and in the way her writing changes according to the nature of her readings. The style of "Coming to Writing," an essay which followed "The Laugh of the Medusa" by less than a year, is exuberant, polemical, filled with wordplay and parodic inventions rooted in the works of the "masters" (Freud's lecture on "Femininity," for instance, becomes "Requiemth Lecture on the Infeminitesimal").[1] Here sexual difference is directly explored in personal terms, and in opposition to certain cultural, psychoanalytic, religious, and political sources. In comparison, "Clarice Lispector: The Approach," from 1979, shows the influence of Lispector's work in its strikingly meditative tone. Elements from Cixous's earlier work are approached here with a simple, poetic, and ultimately philosophical vocabulary. Ironically, this pared-down vocabulary may be more opaque for the American reader than the complex wordplay

---

1. Interestingly, there are no more references to "Uncle Freud" in the essays that follow. Cixous explains that the unconscious of Lispector's texts is not "populated with Freudian scenes. True, it always takes place 'behind something,' as Clarice says . . . It happens because there is, because there takes place. This place is largely that which would be delimited by the range of the body: within reach of the hand, ear, or the senses." Hélène Cixous, foreword to *The Stream of Life,* by Clarice Lispector, trans. Elizabeth Lowe and Earl Fitz (Minneapolis: University of Minnesota Press, 1989), p. xxxiv. Why Lispector's texts *are* populated with Heideggerian scenes is a question that points to the theatrical specificity of Cixous's use of the word "scene." Heidegger is not so much a pertinent theoretical source for Lispector's work as he is a phantom-actor on the stage of her creations.

of "Coming to Writing." The subject of sexual difference is difficult to locate in a line like this one from the beginning of the essay: "Loving the true of the living, what seems *ungrateful* to narcissus eyes, the nonprestigious, the non-immediate, loving the origin, interesting oneself personally with the impersonal, with the animal, with the thing." And yet, through a careful reading of the subsequent text, one comes equipped with new resources to the question formulated without fanfare in the final passage: "And woman?" The text is structured like an enigma.

The third and fourth essays in this collection, "Tancredi Continues" and "The Last Painting or the Portrait of God," were both published in 1983. They show Cixous's interest in the sources and motivating forces of artistic work in genres not limited to writing. Unlike much literary work on the arts in the United States, however, Cixous's interest in music and the visual arts remains tied to the figurative, to the language of the story in its different vocabularies. "The Last Painting or the Portrait of God" takes as its point of departure Clarice Lispector's fascination with the instant ("Each thing has an instant in which it is. I want to take possession of the thing's *is*.") to explore differences between the gestures of writing and painting. One such difference lies in the possibility of "fidelity" to the instant, a concept that could be confused with realism but that is more accurately approached as the problem of making figurative the "vision" of the writer. What the painter makes visible, the writer offers to the imaging capacities of the reader: "I am the awkward sorceress of the invisible: my sorcery is powerless to evoke, without the help of your sorcery. Everything I evoke depends on you, depends on your trust, your faith." "Fidelity" is also illustrated here in terms of the cultural permission (or lack of it) to "contemplate a woman's real nudity" in writing.

The other piece from 1983 is "Tancredi Continues," a fragment of a longer, unpublished fiction called *Jerusalem Continues,* which Cixous wrote in 1981–82. This is her reading of Tasso's epic *Jerusalem Delivered* and Gioacchino Rossini's opera version, *Tancredi.* The intensely poetic language of this text condenses several kinds of struggles and several kinds of bodies into one space: the poetic space of contested Jerusalem. Two camps fight over (the gender of) this "beloved body." On one level they are religious/national camps (this is one of the first works to reveal Cixous's growing interest in the problematic of nationalities), but Cixous's use of the startling gender portrayals of Tasso's epic highlights them above all as the camps of the two sexes, in their lethal, passionate dispute over the masculinity or femininity of the body of the beloved.

The last two essays, from 1989, represent Cixous's most recent work on Clarice Lispector. The brief "By the Light of an Apple" serves as a prelude to the final essay in this collection, "The Author in Truth." It plays on the title of a novel by Clarice Lispector, *The Apple in the Dark,* to convey Lispector's illuminating force: she is the "Watchwoman, night-light of the world." Cixous compares Lispector with Kafka, Rilke, Rimbaud, and Heidegger, but only on conditional feminine terms: *if* Kafka had been a woman, Rilke a Jewish Brazilian, Rimbaud a mother, Heidegger the author of a Romance of the Earth. Despite the murmurings of philosophers "in her forests," Lispector is a writer who "knows nothing," because her work is not the stasis of cognition; it is the journey of "re-cognition." As such, her work "puts us back in the worldschool" of unceasing,

"equal" attention. For Cixous, the political quality of Lispector's work lies in the absence of a hierarchy of artistic
objects. ("Political" in a qualified sense, clearly; Cixous asks
the question whether *The Hour of the Star* is a political text,
and answers: "Subreptitiously. If there is a politics of
spirituality.")

In "The Author in Truth," Cixous plunges into the question of identification between reader, author, and character.
She proceeds with all the complexity of Bakhtinian analysis
of speech acts, but without a specialized theoretical vocabulary. The class position of the character Macabea is at the
heart of the identificatory labyrinth in *The Hour of the Star:*
"We, character, reader, author, circulate between 'I am not
her,' and 'I could be her,' as we advance along the most
powerful path of meditation that we can take in thinking of
the other." Here we find echoing in "The Author in Truth"
the same question of the reader's position that reverberates
in *"Coming to Writing" and Other Essays* as a whole.

The opening paragraphs of the title essay locate the problematic of reading as a heartbeat-like trace audible inside as
well as outside the text. The initial "I" who narrates is the
child-reader who scans the Face—the Face as the maternal
geography that is the signature of life for the infant. The
child's act of reading is as inevitable as her primal attraction
to the (m)other: the other signifies; the child reads. Reading
the Face is necessary for the child in order to keep the
connection with the other alive, and in fact to keep the
other alive at all, since otherness denotes existence *in relation
to* the subject. The Face serves also as a beacon of light that
makes it possible to name the shadowy world around the
child. In the relationship to this other, the child-narrator is

at once the most helpless and most powerful of readers—depending on the other, and creating the other. Hélène Cixous pointed out in the recent colloquium "Readings of Sexual Difference" at the International College of Philosophy that in the act of reading, one chooses one's subject of reading; and in doing so, one becomes the author of the reading. So reading is a not-quite-authorized coming to writing. In this way, the reader of "Coming to Writing" coincides with the elusive narrator on her dizzying trail through the forest.

The narrator of "Coming to Writing" is herself unable to authorize her writing until the *"souffle"*—most simply, the breath, the intake of life, but also the current of inspiration—sets her body in motion and inscribes her desire in the flesh. By then, it is too late to turn back; the body *will* function as a source. Cixous has described the woman-body as the "place from which": from which birth occurs, metaphorically and organically, from which the passage is made from the inside to the outside, from which a new body emerges to read otherness in its turn.[2] In this text Cixous's fascination with, and her gratitude for, sources, makes the question of writing into a celebration of its places of emission and its places of incorporation. On her journey to and through the "places from which," she sends a stream

---

2. I translate *corps de femme* as "woman-body" rather than "woman's body" to indicate that it can be read as a construct as well as an irreducible, in keeping with the subtlety of Cixous's usage of terms like "woman" and "feminine." While the term *corps de femme* is anchored in the organicity of the female body, the male body can also function as a "place from which," as Cixous suggests repeatedly in works such as "Tancredi Continues," *The Indiad,* and so on. The female body is the place from which metaphors of femininity originate, but it has no copyright to them.

of correspondence, her "Letters from the Life-Watch," and other bodily chronicles.

To achieve her readings of life, Cixous practices a politics/poetics of attention articulated through her readings of the work of Clarice Lispector. Compared to "Coming to Writing," which is often as vigorous and wet as a newborn struggling for its first breath, or as a fish splashing in water, "Clarice Lispector: The Approach" is composed with philosophical restraint, panther steps, respect for the fragility of an egg. That is because the interventions of this essay are directed to a stage of life in which the urgency of reading the Face has been forgotten, and in which we allow what Cixous refers to as the media forcibly to read us, the erstwhile reader. "We are living in the time of the flat thought-screen, of newspaper-thinking, which does not leave time to think the littlest thing according to its living mode. We must save the approach that opens and leaves space for *the other*." In this jaded time we are, passively, the "other" of the advertising executive, for instance. By contrast, in the world-readings of Clarice Lispector, "names are hands she lays on space, with a tenderness so intense that at last smiles a face, o you."

This tender naming, and its ability to coax the face into bloom, is the product of a patience, a reserve, an attention, that Cixous characterizes as soul. "Soul" is one of many terms that are generally banished to the metaphysical broom closet these days but that Cixous gifts with a reincarnation, in the sense of a reconstituted relationship to the body. The soul for her is an ultrasensual substance: "The soul is the magic of attention. And the body of the soul is made from a fine, fine ultrasensual substance, so finely sensitive that it can pick up the murmur of every hatching, the infinitesimal music of particles calling to one another to compose themselves in fragrance." This reading-soul is inseparable from the experience of the senses, but it is not conflated with the senses: it is a sensory/sensual attention. A sensist capacity for reading. A sensualism of readings via the senses.

The reading-soul raises the question of the politics of poetic rhetoric. Cixous takes on the trope of the rose: Is a woman a rose or is a woman a woman? Do we know a woman best as a rose or as a woman? When does a rose become a mask for woman, and vice versa? This touches on the question of the mimetic relation between text and object, which, like the question of masculinity or femininity in its relation to the body, is not easily resolved in Cixous's work, or in Lispector's work. (Lispector's story "The Imitation of the Rose" can be read, for instance, as the mad radicality of mimetic structure in the religious classic *The Imitation of Christ* when applied to the housewife and her sanctum, the domestic environment.) The attention Lispector applies to the organic is not so much a transformational logic as a respect that explores the form of its object, that tries to greet each "species" with an attention of a similar "species." And so when she considers that archipoetic object, the rose, she might examine its elements by replacing it with a turtle, a cockroach, an oyster; whereas Rilke "could replace it only with a unicorn," or "in lacework."

But what prevents this approach from turning into a mimetic code is the strict ambiguity of Cixous's use of terms such as "species" in the first place. In "The Author in Truth" she writes, "Yes, Clarice's project is to make the other human subject appear equal—and this is positive—to the roach. Each to her own species." The roach (which is far from anthropomorphized in *The Passion*) and the human subject as mimetic partners? Clearly, realism is not at the bottom of this mystery. Cixous suggests a comparison of Gertrude Stein's approach to the rose with Lispector's. Stein's "A rose is a rose is a rose . . . " is subversive "hyperlinguistics." Through repetition, Stein reveals "the fact that the signifier always represses." Lispector, on the other hand, presents a "story" of the rose, of which "'I write you this facsimile' is one of the definitions."[3] But there are always further definitions of the rose (other than that of the inevitable facsimilitude of representation) which have to do with the rose's organic life. In the end, imitation in Cixous's work has less to do with mimesis than with the mimosa, the flower that takes its name from the Latin botanical term *mimus*.

Listening with the "ultrasensual substance of the soul," the writer reads the object into existence. And so woman is represented not only as the story of a historical, literary facsimile, with which all feminists are familiar, a rose-text, but as a body to be explored. This body belongs to character, author, and reader. Cixous rediscovers Lispector through the eyes of Macabea, for instance, and catches a glimpse of her own double: "Reading this narrative I sometimes almost forgot her, I did forget her. Later I remembered. And for one second, through Macabea's eyes, I saw Clarice Lispector heavily made up, coming out of the salon where having her hair done had cost a month's worth of sausage sandwiches. Or was it myself I saw?"

3. Hélène Cixous, foreword to *The Stream of Life,* by Clarice Lispector, p. xv.

The reader author-izes a reading, the writer reads woman into writing, the reader becomes writer, the writer becomes reader—in which direction are we going? In French, the word *sens* signifies both "meaning" and "direction." And in French, the titles of the first three essays in this book all contain terms of movement that can be read in more than one meaning-direction at a time. "La Venue à l'écriture" hinges on the various possible meanings of *la venue:* the path of growth or development, the coming (as in "the advent"), or the (feminine) one who has arrived. (*La venue* is also a homophone of *l'avenue*.) The syntax of "L'Approche de Clarice Lispector" suggests either "Clarice Lispector's Approach," or, on the contrary, "Approaching Clarice Lispector." It could even be read as "The Approach—from (the Point of Departure of) Clarice Lispector." In "Tancredi Continues," the lack of an object for the verb "continues" leaves the reader to wonder: what, where, and whom does Tancredi continue to do, go, and be? Does all this circulation simply lead the reader in the direction of movement for the sake of avoiding stasis, and if so, what does this have to do with "truth," as in "The Author in Truth?"

"Truth" is a term of movement as it relates to the constantly self-displacing yet ultimately irreducible nature of the author's signature, the trace of the body writing. For Cixous, the signature of the author tells the whole story of *The Hour of the Star* and its multiply impoverished heroine, Macabea: "I, Rodrigo S.M., I am in truth Clarice Lispector put in parentheses, and only the author '(in truth Clarice Lispector)' can approach this beginning of a woman. This is the impossible truth. It is *the inexpressible, indemonstrable truth,* which can be said only in parentheses . . . It is the truth, a woman, beating like a heart, in the parenthesis of life." In the parenthetical truth of the creation of the female character by the female author within the male narrator lies a mystery: "The identity of the 'I' who cannot answer." In witnessing existence in the parentheses of the text, Cixous seeks freedom from the confining authorizations of names: "We are much more than what our own name authorizes us and obligates us to believe we are. . . . We are possible. Anyone. We need only avoid closing up the parentheses in which our 'why-nots' live."

Our "why-nots" are often the unprivileged, who are often women. In "Coming to Writing," Cixous describes an idealized vision of what a writing-voyage would be for the elite: "for this elite, the gorgeous journey without horizon, beyond everything, the appalling yet intoxicating excursion toward the never-yet-said." But for woman, devoured by "the jealous Wolf, your ever-insatiable grand-mother," there is the "vocation of the swallowed up, voyage of the scybalum." In a social structure hungry to consume them, women are limited to the voyage of the digestive tract, to literal incorporation. The world of the fairy tale is a maze of lost paths filled with dangerous encounters: "For the daughters of the housewife: the straying into the forest." In this forest, the wolf is the site of the legendary struggle with the enigma: "Instead of the great enigmatic duel with the Sphinx, the dangerous questioning addressed to the body of the Wolf: What is the body for? Myths end up having our hides. Logos opens its great maw, and swallows us whole."

But in the writing-voyage, the (domestic) forest reso-nates as more than the haunted site of the fairy tale. It is also the paradigm for the *"Claricewege,"* Cixous's adaptation of the Heideggerian *Holzwege* to Lispector's writing: "Thinking according to Clarice, I immediately come to think of Heidegger and his *Holzwege:* 'Trails in the wood, trails that lead nowhere, that trail.'" The *Holzweg* has, significantly, been used to pinpoint the end of philosophy, the point at which it no longer moves ahead. Louis Althusser claimed that the only possible contemporary philosophy would be theoretical discourse *on* philosophy, because philosophy had become limited to "a path leading nowhere, a '*Holzweg.*'"[4] But for Cixous, the Claricean *Holzweg* allows the reader to live the path as source. "The Clarice-voice gives us the ways. A fear takes hold of us. Calls us: 'There are nothing but ways.' Gives-takes our hand. A deeply moved, clairvoyant fear—we take it. Leads us. We *make* ways." The trails that trail give the gift of the present in its infinity of possible forms; they teach vulnerability to "the two great lessons of living: slowness and ugliness." Entering the forest of the *Claricewege,* the writing body is the subject of a movement that is not *logomotion* but love of motion, trust of fear, trust of slowness. In the dark trails, we encounter Hélène Cixous, a philosopher—in Red Riding Hood's clothing—of an ongoing feminine tradition. She helps the reader make her way to the question: What is the reader in truth?

Translating the resonant poetics of Hélène Cixous's work into anything but her particular language—which is not French, not German, but poetry—is a difficult (Pro-

---

4. Luc Ferry and Alain Renaut, *French Philosophy of the Sixties: An Essay on Antihumanism,* trans. Mary Schnackenberg Cattani (Amherst: University of Massachusetts Press, 1990), pp. 4–5.

methean?) task in which the reader must participate for full effect. The gathering connotative force of Cixous's word-play resists any word-for-word equivalence.

And no truly appropriate explanatory apparatus has ever been found for poetry. Endnotes are one way of documenting the necessarily unstable process of translation, which Barbara Johnson has called "an exercise in violent approximation."[5] However, since endnotes do interrupt the musical flow of the text, I have tried to minimize their intervention.

Among previous translators of her work, Betsy Wing in *The Newly Born Woman* chose to render words that were "too full of sense" in the original through "a process of accretion" in the translation.[6] Yet the explicit presentation of a series of terms in answer to the poetic multiplicity of one term bypasses the relationship between the reader and the French text, in which several meanings may be called into action at once or allowed to lie dormant. The present translators have more frequently chosen a one-to-one relationship of the English terms to the French, although these terms may function simply as signposts to other possible readings. In the end, it is hoped the reader of this collection will accept the author's invitation to lend it a little "soul."

I want to thank Sarah Cornell, Ann Liddle, and Susan Sellers for their translations, and Marguerite Sandré for her

5. Jacques Derrida, *Dissemination,* trans. Barbara Johnson (Chicago: University of Chicago Press, 1981), p. xviii: "To translate an author so excruciatingly aware of the minutest linguistic difference is an exercise in violent approximation."

6. Hélène Cixous and Catherine Clément, *The Newly Born Woman,* trans. Betsy Wing (Minneapolis: University of Minnesota Press, 1986), p. 163.

resourcefulness in this international project. I am also grateful to Susan Suleiman for her insightful suggestions and to Maria Ascher for her exceptional editing. Finally, I want to thank Hélène Cixous for her patient and illuminating comments.

# Notes

## 1. Coming to Writing

1. *"Du point de vue de l'oeil d'âme. L'oeil dame."* The juxtaposition of the homophones *d'âme* ("of the soul") and *dame* ("woman" or "lady") following the expression *point de vue* ("point of view"), creates a connection between the soul's vision and woman's vision, translated here as "the eye of a womansoul."—*Editor*

2. *"Terreur: l'arrêt de vie, l'arrêt de mort."* The word *arrêt* ("stop") is a homonym in French, and can be translated both as "arrest" and "sentence"; here, "life arrest, death sentence."—*Editor*

3. *"Mon refus de la maladie comme arme. Il y a une même qui me fait horreur. N'est-elle pas déjà morte? Sa maladie: c'est le cancer. Une main malade. Elle est elle-même la maladie."* In this passage Cixous employs a characteristic form of wordplay: usage of the pronoun *elle* to refer interchangeably to more than one noun, including both fictional female subjects and things that are feminine nouns in French. Here the feminine nouns for "sickness" and "hand" overlap with the identification of a feminine self—*une même*—and this plurality of reference leaves the reader uncertain as to whether *elle* indicates that the sickness or the woman is already dead (*déjà morte*), whether the hand or the woman is the source of the sickness (*elle-même la maladie*), and so on.—*Editor*

4. *"Tu as deux mains. Tu as demain."* In this passage on the rejection of sickness as a weapon, the echo of the homophones *deux mains* ("two hands") and *demain* ("tomorrow") creates the suggestion that even if one hand does not work, the other remains a resource, like the future.—*Editor*

5. *"On tue une fille."* The title of this passage echoes the title of Freud's essay "A Child is Being Beaten."—*Editor*

6. *"Peut pas s'empêcher de voler!"* / *"En ce cas, nous avons des cages extra."* The verb *voler* means both "to fly" and "to steal." In this scene, a young girl irrepressibly steals—apparently language, in this case—and simultaneously flies (from the scene of the crime, in a flight of words). She is then punished with "special cages," meaning not only prison for the thief, but foot-binding to restrain the mobility of the girl who "flies." See Nancy Kline's introduction to *The Tongue Snatchers,* by Claudine Herrmann, for a gloss on Cixous's development of this term.—*Editor*

7. *"Le souffle 'veut' une forme."* The word *souffle* means both "breath" and spirit, as in *le souffle créateur,* "the breath of God." It is also used to indicate inspiration, as in *avoir du souffle,* "to be inspired." Throughout this passage (and elsewhere in Cixous's work, such as the 1975 fiction *Souffles*), the vocabulary of breathing, or respiration, is aligned with a parallel vocabulary of inspiration.—*Editor*

8. Søren Kierkegaard, *The Diary of a Seducer,* trans. Gerd Gillhoff (New York: Frederick Ungar, 1966), pp. 161–162.

9. *"Souris! J'entre: souris."* The images of the narrator as mouse and God as the "good lord cat" converge here through the homonym *souris. Souris* denotes both the noun "mouse" and the singular imperative of the verb "to smile": God smiles, and the narrator enters the mousehole of his mouth.—*Editor*

10. *"L'âmant."* The circumflex added to the letter "a" in *amant* ("lover") introduces the phoneme *âme* (soul) into the word "lover."—*Editor*

11. *"Ma lalemande!"* This is Cixous's child's-ear version of the French word for "German" (*l'allemand*): spelled phonetically and made feminine (*lalemande*), it contains a near homophone of the word *amande* ("almond"). In this way, Cixous's mother tongue becomes a source of nourishment: *Mon aliment.* (Wordplay with *amande* is also widespread in Cixous's 1988 novel *Manne.*) Likewise, *languelait* is a phonetic spelling of *l'anglais* ("English"), which produces a pun combining *langue* ("language") and *lait* ("milk").—*Editor*

12. Stéphane Mallarmé, "Brise Marine," in *Oeuvres complètes,* ed. Henri Mondor and G. Jean-Aubry (Paris: Gallimard, 1945), p. 38.

13. *"L'Empire du Propre, du Pire en Pire de la Propriété."* This expression is

particularly difficult to translate, since in English there is no one equivalent of *propre* in its dual function of adjective and noun. Among its numerous meanings are "clean," "suitable," "own," "a distinctive feature," "a particularity." *L'Empire du Propre* has been rendered by Betsy Wing in *The Newly Born Woman* as "The Empire of the Selfsame," which recalls Gillian C. Gill's translation of *la loi du même* in Luce Irigaray's *Speculum of the Other Woman*, as "the law of the self-same." "Self-same" in Irigaray's text refers to Freud's reduction of the libido to the desire "the phallus feels for the phallus"; here, the term *Propre*, echoed by *Propriété*, most directly evokes social hegemonies of possession and the divisive force of appropriation. From *Empire* Cixous takes the syllable *Pire* ("worst") and the near homophone *en Pire;* in the expression *du Pire en Pire* ("from Bad to Worse") one can hear "the worst empire."—*Editor*

14. *"Pas d'autre Avant que, dans l'ambigüité, ce qui avait eu lieu avant?"* *Avant* can be read as "forward" or "before"; this repetition evokes the paradox of a forward movement which is indistinguishable from that which took place before.—*Editor*

15. *"Avec Cixous, les imbéciles font des sous."* A *sou* was formerly a five-centime coin in French currency. Cixous's wordplay suggests that imbeciles capitalize (*faire des sous*, "to make money") on her name by punning on the slang term for minimal amounts of money, *des sous.*—*Editor*

16. *"C'est en les regardant s'accoucher que j'ai appris à aimer les femmes."* The verb *accoucher* (to give birth) is italicized and made reflexive here, suggesting that when women give birth, they are both the subject and the object of their act.—*Editor*

17. *"Les femmes, on sait ce que c'est. Moi, j'en ai une, depuis trente ans."* The word *femme* means both "woman" and "wife" in French. The Superuncle correspondingly equates knowledge of women with possession of a wife.—*Editor*

18. *"J'ai une animâle."* The masculine word *animal* is transformed through the addition of the feminine definite article *une* and the feminine ending *-e;* the gender play becomes more elaborate with the metamorphosis of the final syllable *mal* into *mâle* (male). This hybrid "animale" is the first identification in a menagerie of metaphors for irrepressible feminine sexuality. The subsequent animal

components of this scene of shifting and multiple sexuality—*"C'est une espèce de chamoi, un moiseau ou une moiselle"*—are linguistically inseparable from the "self" or the "ego" (*le moi*). The word *chamoi* is an invention which plays on the phonetic conjunction of *chat* ("cat") and *moi* ("me/ego"). It is also a homophone of *chamois* (a small, goat-like antelope), and a near-homophone of *chameau* ("camel"). The terms *moiseau* and *moiselle* echo the feminine noun *demoiselle* ("young lady") and its masculine equivalent *demoiseau*, while also combining *moi* and *oiseau/oiselle* (the masculine and feminine words for "bird").

The title of this scene, and its evocation of forbidden masturbatory pleasures, possibly allude to Rousseau's *Confessions*; but here, the playful depiction of the female genitalia (signified by the word *con* in vulgar French) marks this "confession" as specifically feminine.—*Editor*

19. This passage parodies Freud's "Lecture 33: Femininity." The title of Cixous's passage in French, "Requième Conférence sur l'Infiminité," plays on three words: *l'infime* ("the minuscule" or "the infinitesimal"), *l'infini* ("the infinite"), and, of course, *féminité* ("femininity"). Cixous uses a French translation as a point of departure; the English translation by Lytton Strachey in *New Introductory Lectures on Pyschoanalysis* (New York: Norton, 1933) begins, "Ladies and Gentlemen,—All the while I am preparing to talk to you I am struggling with an internal difficulty." The form of the French introductory address is retained here because of the suggested absorption of the feminine into the masculine: *"Messieurs-messieurs, Mesdames-messieurs."*—*Editor*

20. *"Pas d'hommicile fixe."* Cixous's altered spelling of the term *domicile fixe* ("permanent residence") to include the syllable *d'homme* ("of man") parodies the masculine quality of terms denoting establishment; the litany of which this term is a part includes "fatherland" and "history."—*Editor*

21. *"Au plus près d'Elle, notre mère la plus puissante."* The capitalization of the pronoun indicating the feminine noun *la mort* ("death") emphasizes the feminine identification of death. Death is discussed here in conjunction with the feminine noun *la vie* ("life"), and the pronoun *elle* is used inextricably for both nouns in the context of the "desire

for both extremes to meet"; in this way, death is "our double mother."—*Editor*

22. *"Elle est même* la *retenue, socialement."* Accompanied by the definite article *la,* the feminine word *retenue* can be read as both "restraint itself" and "the one who is restrained," to indicate that these two social positions are often conflated.—*Editor*

23. *"Toujours l'éclat de l'être qui me donne le Là."* Here the expression *donner le la,* "to set the tone," is combined with the word *là,* which can signify either "there" or "here," consistent with the mystery of the internal/external cite of the source.—*Editor*

24. *"Une de mes vies me ramène toujours à bon corps."* A bon corps, translated here as "to solid body," is a variation on *à bon port* ("to safe harbor").—*Editor*

25. *"Je l'ai payé chair."* Cixous's spelling of the expression *payer cher* (to pay dearly) as *payer chair* indicates a payment of the "flesh" (*chair*). —*Editor*

26. See Hélène Cixous, *Inside,* trans. Carol Barko (New York: Schocken Books, 1984). Published in French as *Dedans* by Grasset (1969) and Des Femmes (1986).

27. Hélène Cixous, *Souffles* (Paris: Des Femmes, 1975).

28. Hélène Cixous, *Troisième Corps* (Paris: Grasset, 1970).


## 2. *Clarice Lispector: The Approach*

1. Clarice Lispector, *A Paixao Segundo C.L.* [The Passion According to C.L.] (Rio de Janeiro: José Olympio, 1974), my translation, emphasis added.

   "According to" is *second* in Brazilian. And in French, the signifier *second* signifies both coming second, and coming to someone's aid. One passion seconds the other, G.H. "seconds" the passion of C.L., who in turn comes to seek us and in turn goes back up the apocalyptic path with us. G.H.: what is left of C.L. at the end of this long and pitiless pleasure. G.H. or C.L.: no longer initials, once the dispossession of the self is accomplished, but atoms designating the being who ventured out into this region of the Least, where Hölderlin, scout of the strange, also went to sojourn.

2. See Clarice Lispector, *The Stream of Life,* trans. Elizabeth Lowe and Earl Fitz (Minneapolis: University of Minnesota Press, 1989).

3. Thinking according to Clarice, I immediately come to think of Heidegger and his *Holzwege:* "Trails in the wood, trails that lead nowhere, that trail."

   Then it follows that my German tongue mixes with my French tongue. In German, *Obst* signifies "fruit," or "fruits." *Lesen:* "reading."

4. Martin Heidegger, "Lecture 9," in *What Is Called Thinking?* trans. J. Glenn Gray (New York: Harper and Row, 1968), p. 208.

5. Martin Heidegger, "Das Wort," in *Unterwegs zur Sprache* (Tübingen: Neske, 1975), p. 233. [Cixous has chosen to play with the German language precisely at the point where it resists translation. In doing so, she stresses the singular force of each language.—*Editor*]

6. She lets-be: and at each now, giving itself to be gathered/read from her *souffle* ("breath," "inspiration"), there is. Response to the seminar of J. Derrida, who questions the possibility of "Giving (oneself) the Time," Clarice gives the time(s). Is entirely welcome, response, giving receptivity. Makes the giving-receiving possible.

7. Clarice Lispector, "The Egg and the Chicken," in *The Foreign Legion: Stories and Chronicles,* trans. Giovanni Pontiero (Manchester, England: Carcanet, 1986), p. 54.

8. Heidegger, "Das Wesen der Sprache," in *Unterwegs zur Sprache,* p. 193.

9. As for this event, if one wanted to translate the work of Clarice into Derrida's language, perhaps one might hear something like the following: the adventuality of the event proper to the work is that it be, rather than not be, and this adventuality of the event is in itself what the work consists of in the work of art. What seems proper or essential to a work is its truth as event—the event of the event—through which something is, that was not previously, originates: the egg, that previously was not, is. What the egg work sets to egg work is the event that caused it to be, and the unicity of this event, its one and only egg time, keeps itself in the egg work and there institutes truth as the work in the guise of the egg of art.

   [*"Ce que l'œufvre met en œufvre."* The artistic "adventuality"—a combination of "advent" and "eventuality"—of the egg is reflected in Cixous's wordplay here: the word *œuf,* meaning "egg," is integrated into the word *œuvre,* allowing us to speak of the *œufvre,* the egg work.—*Editor*]

10. Lispector, "The Egg and the Chicken," p. 47. And for Heidegger, it is when the soothsayer (*Seber*) has seen that he truly sees. "Only when a man has seen does he truly see. To see is to have seen. What is seen has arrived and remains for him in sight. A seer has always already seen. Having seen in advance he sees into the future. He sees the future tense out of the perfect. When the poet speaks of the seer's seeing as a having-seen, he must say what the seer has seen in the pluperfect tense: *ede,* he had seen. What is it that the seer has seen in advance? Obviously, only what becomes present in the lightning that penetrates his sight. What is seen in such a seeing can only be what comes to presence in unconcealment." Martin Heidegger, "The Anaximander Fragment," in *Early Greek Thinking* (New York: Harper and Row, 1975), p. 34.

   But for Clarice—"My foresight closed the world to me" (Lispector, *Passion,* p. 9)—in order to "see" the egg, it is necessary to "unsee": to try not to crush the egg with a hasty glance [*coup d'oeil; coup* also signifies "blow"—*Editor*], not to see-swallow it. But to wait for the hour when the egg, foiling all watching, will make its way to the tranquil, disinterested, open waiting that lets it come forth or not, according to its own mode. Sometimes the egg arrives (but something entirely different may happen; or nothing at all).

11. Lispector, *Egg,* p. 47.

12. Clarice Lispector, *The Passion According to G.H.,* trans. Ronald W. Sousa (Minneapolis: University of Minnesota Press, 1988), p. 13.

13. Ibid., p. 7.

14. Lispector, *Stream,* p. 62.

15. Ibid., p. 58.

16. Lispector, *Passion,* p. 43.

17. See Clarice Lispector, "The Imitation of the Rose," in *Family Ties,* trans. Giovanni Pontiero (Austin: University of Texas Press, 1972), pp. 53–72.

18. R. M. Rilke, *The Notebooks of Malte Laurids Brigge,* trans. M. D. Herter Norton (New York: Norton, 1964), p. 109. "It was in the year after Mama's death that I first noticed Abelone. Abelone was

always there, and one used her up as best one could. But all at once I asked myself: Why is Abelone here? Everyone in our house had a reason to be there, even if it was not always as obvious as, for example, the utility of Sophie Oxe. But why was Abelone there?"

19. Heidegger, "Anaximander," p. 53.
20. Lispector, *Stream,* p. 70.
21. Lispector, *Passion,* pp. 12–13.
22. Lispector, *Stream,* p. 19.
23. Lispector, *Passion,* p. 11.
24. Lispector, *Stream,* pp. 43–44.
25. Ibid., p. 50.

### *3. Tancredi Continues*

1. William Shakespeare, *Twelfth Night,* act 1, scene 5.

### *4. The Last Painting or the Portrait of God*

1. Claude Monet, letter to Gustave Geffroy, in *Claude Monet at the Time of Giverny,* ed. Jacqueline and Maurice Guillaud (Paris: Guillaud, 1983), p. 80.
2. Clarice Lispector, *The Stream of Life,* trans. Elizabeth Lowe and Earl Fitz (Minneapolis: University of Minnesota Press, 1989), p. 3.
3. Lispector, *Stream,* p. 4.
4. Monet, letter to Alice Hoschedé, in *At the Time of Giverny,* p. 27.
5. *The Complete Letters of Vincent Van Gogh,* vol. 2 (Greenwich: New York Graphic Society, n.d.), p. 204. Cixous has slightly modified this translation.—*Editor*
6. Monet, letter to Alice Hoschedé, in *At the Time of Giverny,* p. 36.
7. Journal of Julie Manet, in *At the Time of Giverny,* p. 36.
8. Monet, letter to Gustave Geffroy, in *At the Time of Giverny,* p. 80.
9. *The Complete Letters of Vincent Van Gogh,* vol. 2, p. 590.
10. Ibid., p. 596.
11. Ibid., pp. 598–599.
12. Paul Cézanne, quoted by Joachim Gasquet, in *At the Time of Giverny,* p. 208.
13. See Clarice Lispector, "Such Gentleness," in *Soulstorm: Stories by*

*Clarice Lispector,* trans. Alexis Levitin (New York: New Directions, 1989), pp. 160–161.

14. See Clarice Lispector, *The Passion According to G.H.,* trans. Ronald W. Sousa (Minneapolis: University of Minnesota Press, 1988).

15. *Le Fou de peinture: Hokusai et son temps,* exhibition catalog, Centre Culturel du Marais (Paris: CRES, 1980), p. 217.

16. A. Houbraken, in Horst Gerson, *Rembrandt et son oeuvre* (Paris: Hachette, 1968), p. 466.

17. Monet, letter to Alice Hoschedé, in *At the Time of Giverny,* p. 33, emphasis added.

18. *The Complete Letters of Vincent Van Gogh,* vol. 3, p. 187.

19. Monet, in *At the Time of Giverny,* p. 198.

20. Wassily Kandinsky, in *At the Time of Giverny,* p. 80.

21. Oskar Kokoschka, in Gerson, *Rembrandt et son oeuvre,* p. 478.

22. Unpublished notebooks by Clarice Lispector, cited in Olga Borelli, *Clarice Lispector: Esboço para um possível retrato* (Rio de Janeiro: Editora Nova Fronteira, 1981), p. 77.

23. Ibid., p. 77.

24. *Le Fou de peinture,* p. 376.

25. Clarice Lispector, in Borelli, *Clarice Lispector,* p. 21.

26. Monet, letter to Alice Hoschedé, in *At the Time of Giverny,* p. 31.

27. *Le Fou de peinture,* p. 361.

## 6. The Author in Truth

1. See Hélène Cixous, *Limonade tout était si infini* (Paris: Editions des Femmes, 1982).

2. Franz Kafka, "Aus den Gesprächblättern," in *Briefe, 1902–1924* (New York: Schocken Books, 1958), p. 491.

3. Clarice Lispector, *A Hora da Estrela* [The Hour of the Star] (São Paulo: José Olympio, 1979), p. 13, my translation. [All excerpts from *A Hora da Estrela* in this essay have been translated by Cixous so as to convey the startling rhythms and irregular syntax that characterize Lispector's work; for a discussion of Lispector's prose style, see Cixous's foreword to *The Stream of Life,* by Clarice Lispector, trans. Elizabeth Lowe and Earl Fitz (Minneapolis: University of Minnesota Press, 1989), pp. xxxi–xxxii. The word "Cordel" in

the next to last "title" in this passage, "A Teargas-like Story of a Cordel," is the term for the Brazilian popular ballads sold in markets, ballads which always tell sad stories.—*Editor*]

4. Lispector, *A Hora da Estrela*, p. 7.

5. Ibid., emphasis added.

6. "Cène Primitive": For an elaboration of this term, see Hélène Cixous, "Reaching the Point of Wheat, or A Portrait of the Artist as a Maturing Woman," *New Literary History* 19 (1987–1988): 2. "I'd like you also to consider the primitive scene in the way we would write the word *cène* in French without an *s;* without an *s,* it means 'the meal.' 'The primitive scene' is also 'the primitive meal.' "—*Editor*

7. Lispector, *A Hora da Estrela*, p. 26.

8. Ibid., p. 22.

9. Ibid., p. 7.

10. Ibid.

11. See Clarice Lispector, *Felicidade Clandestina* (Rio de Janeiro: Nova Fronteira, 1971).

12. See Clarice Lispector, *The Apple in the Dark,* trans. Gregory Rabassa (Austin: University of Texas Press, 1961).

13. Clarice Lispector, "The Foreign Legion," in *The Foreign Legion: Stories and Chronicles,* trans. Giovanni Pontiero (Manchester, England: Carcanet, 1986), pp. 89–90.

14. Clarice Lispector, *The Passion According to G.H.,* trans. Ronald W. Sousa (Minneapolis: University of Minnesota Press, 1988), p. 164. Sousa translates *homem* as "person" instead of "man." See Lispector, *A Paixao Segundo C.L.* [The Passion to C.L.] (Rio de Janeiro: José Olympio, 1974), p. 205.

15. Ibid., p. 163.

16. Ibid., p. 164.

17. Franz Kafka, "Reflections on Sin, Suffering, Hope, and the True Way," in *Dearest Father: Stories and Other Writings* (New York: Schocken Books, 1954), p. 48.

18. Ibid., p. 48.

19. Clarice Lispector, "Such Gentleness," in *Soulstorm: Stories by Clarice Lispector,* trans. Alexis Levitin (New York: New Directions, 1989), p. 160.

20. Ibid., p. 161. Levitin abbreviates the phrase *ponto de trigo* ("point of wheat") as "point."—*Editor*

21. See Lispector, *Stream.*

22. See Clarice Lispector, "Vengeance and Painful Reconciliation," in *The Foreign Legion,* pp. 193–196.

23. See Clarice Lispector, "Mineirinho," in *The Foreign Legion,* pp. 212–215.

24. Lispector, *A Hora da Estrela,* pp. 15–16.

25. Ibid., p. 7.

26. Ibid., p. 48.

27. Ibid., pp. 47–48.

28. Ibid., p. 41.

# Sources

"La Venue à l'écriture": Originally published in *La Venue à l'écriture,* by Hélène Cixous, Madeleine Gagnon, and Annie Leclerc (Paris: Union Générale d'Editions, 10/18, 1977). Collected in *Entre l'écriture* (Paris: Des Femmes, 1986), copyright © 1986 by Editions des Femmes. A portion of the essay, translated by Deborah Jenson, appeared in *The Literary Review* 30 (Spring 1987). The version that appears here was translated by Deborah Jenson, with modifications by Ann Liddle and Susan Sellers.

"L'Approche de Clarice Lispector": Originally published in *Poétique* 40 (November 1979). Collected in *Entre l'écriture* (Paris: Des Femmes, 1986), copyright © 1986 by Editions des Femmes. Translation by Sarah Cornell and Susan Sellers, with modifications by Deborah Jenson.

"Tancrède continue": Originally published in *Etudes Freudiennes* 21–22 (March 1983). Collected in *Entre l'écriture* (Paris: Des Femmes, 1986), copyright © 1986 by Editions des Femmes. The modified translation given here is based on the translation by Ann Liddle and Susan Sellers in *Writing Differences: Readings from the Seminar of Hélène Cixous,* ed. Susan Sellers (Milton Keynes, England: Open University Press, 1988).

"Le Dernier tableau ou le portrait de Dieu": Originally published in *Entre l'écriture* (Paris: Des Femmes, 1986), copyright © 1986 by Edition des Femmes. Translation by Sarah Cornell and Susan Sellers, with modifications by Deborah Jenson.

"A la lumière d'une pomme": Originally published in *L'Heure de Clarice Lispector* (Paris: Des Femmes, 1989), copyright © 1989 by Editions des Femmes. Translation by Deborah Jenson.

"L'Auteur en vérité": Originally presented as a lecture at the Collège Internationale de Philosophie (Paris, 1984). That early version was published in translation as "Extreme Fidelity," in *Writing Differences: Readings*

# Index

Abraham, 151–152
Achilles, 173
Adventuality, 202n9
Amazon, 173
"Animale," 34
Arab, 19
Author, 55, 143–145, 177; author of the, 143; Clarice Lispector, 145, 146, 176, 178–181; cultured, 172; last text of, 136–137; and Macabea, 142; man, 175; masculine, 178, 180; necessary, 138; in reserve, 146; in truth, 145–146, 173, 176, 178, 180; vanquished, 174; what is an, 138; woman, 175
Autobiography-by-proxy, 177

Beethoven, Ludwig van: *Fidelio*, 84
Bible, 18, 29, 149; clandestine, 170; Genesis, 134, 171; on graven image, 3
*Bildungsroman*, 148–149
Birth, 2, 30–31, 52, 71, 179; giving birth to oneself, 28, 43; of the living, 74; Tree of, 45; unhoped-for, 70
Born, 6, 176, 179; of books, 140; newly born woman, 36; things, 61
Breath (*le Souffle*), 10, 16, 31, 32, 71, 136; crises of, 27; as inspiration, 63n6; as origin for writing, 36; outbursts of, 26; *Souffles*, 53; squall of, 31; work of, 30
Burning Bush, 14, 23

Celan, Paul, 148
Cézanne, Paul, 113
Characters, 139, 147, 177, 181
Christianity, 11, 85, 102
Cinderella, 50
Cixous, Hélène, 25–26, 33, 47; *Inside*, 53; *Limonade tout était si infini*, 115, 116, 136; *Souffles*, 53; *Troisième Corps*, 53
Colonies, 17; colonizing and decolonizing, 19
Crusades, 79

Derrida, Jacques, 60, 202n6,9
Difference, 37, 43, 147; circulation of, 27; between human and nonhuman, 31; in language, 22; of the Other, 177; sexual, 23, 102, 157, 173; what is?, 49

Economy, 155; of acceptance, 166; of consolation, 166; of double powerlessness, 165; "feminine," 149–150, 164; instinctual, 56; libidinal, 148; of recognition, 164; "said to be F., said to be M.," 150; of torment, 20
Ego, 24, 113; de-egoization, 156; projection of, 135
Einstein, Albert, 132
Empire of Appropriation (*L'Empire du Propre*), 25; appropriation, 155
English language: and disguise, 15; and gender, 27; and play, 36

Enigma, 6, 81, 101, 127; of the apple, 151; combatant of, 110; high mezzo voice of, 80; painting of, 126; of sources, 10; woman as, 28
Epic, 173–174
Eros, 25
Esau, 152
Essence: and anatomical sex, 155; of face, 66; in her, 175
Eurydice and Orpheus, 49
Eve, 151, 152, 153; and Adam, 25, 149; and apple, 67, 130, 149–153, 176
Evidence, 88; living, 147; star of, 90

Face, the, 1–7, 17, 18, 44, 63, 64, 65, 66, 108
Faith: and Clarice Lispector, 165; as hunger, 164
Faithful, 174; destiny, 94; faithfully, 71; and unfaithful, 78, 172
Fatherland, 15, 36
Feminine, 25, 29, 55, 84, 147, 149, 150, 164, 169, 174; writing, 157
Femininity, 147, 174; genesis of, 151; linguistic repression of, 27; male, 57, 89; overfullness of, 35; poverty and richness in, 177; relationship to oral pleasure, 151; resources of, 31; of a text, 57
Fidelity, 119, 121–122, 127
Fisher King, 153, 154
French language, 13, 16, 22, 148; and flight, 15, 36; and gender, 26; and mother tongue, 28; tongue, 25
Freud, Sigmund, 198n5; "Femininity," 200n19; "Uncle Freud," 51

Gandhi, Mohandas, 132
Gender, 101, 148; determination, 144; in French, 26; law of, 79; without limit, 97; literary, 80; question of, 82
Genet, Jean, 115, 121, 150, 168

German language, 16, 36, 53; and gender, 26–27; Mother, 22; and song, 15, 53
Gift, 62, 65, 163; antigift, 49; and debt, 162, 163, 168; of language, 22; mechanisms of, 162; without return, 49
Gluck, Christoph: *Orpheus*, 83
God, 12, 30, 109, 116, 136, 152, 163, 164; discourse of, 16, 150, 171; "god" as subterfuge, 127; godliness, 41; human gods, 13; if-he-existed, 4; jealousy of, 152; as maternal young man, 17; as mother, 19; mouth of, 18; portrait of, 128–129; sexuality without, 89; sight of, 121; voice of, 171; without, 106; and Word, 18; and writing, 11, 23

Hannukah, 20
Heidegger, Martin, 60, 132; *Early Greek Thinking*, 203n10, 74; *Holzwege*, 202n3; *Unterwegs zur Sprache*, 63, 202n8; *What Is Called Thinking?* 61
History, 6, 7, 17, 43, 47, 76, 87, 149, 174; and bodily inscription, 52; malice of, 93; prehistory, 134; and unconscious, 55; and woman, 71; of women, 27; world, 38, 121
Hokusai, 111, 117, 123, 124, 126, 128, 131
Hölderlin, Friedrich, 60, 201n1
Homer, 173
Horne, Marilyn, 86, 93

James, Henry: *The Aspern Papers*, 46
Jerusalem, 78, 79, 81, 85, 100, 101, 102
Jew, 13; Jewess, 11; Jewish, 12, 17, 59, 99; wandering Jews, 27
Jewoman, 7, 12

Kafka, Franz, 116–117, 132, 136; *Briefe, 1902–1924*, 137; *Dearest Fa-*

*ther: Stories and Other Writings*, 165; "The Metamorphosis," 134
Kandinsky, Wassily, 124
Kierkegaard, Søren: *The Diary of a Seducer*, 17
Kleist, Heinrich von, 173
Kokoschka, Oskar, 125

Language, 12, 20–23, 26, 27, 52, 56, 58, 62, 81, 101, 114, 141, 148, 150
Law, the, 24, 40, 81; absolute, 154; as antipleasure, 154; and the Apple, 150–151; Biblical, 3; guardians of, 11; at stake, 150; woman projected by, 56
Leonardo da Vinci, 48, 116
Lispector, Clarice, 59–77, 104–105, 114–115, 121, 127, 128–129, 132–135; *The Apple in the Dark*, 161; "Clandestine Felicity," 158–160; Clarice-voice, 61; Clarisk, 76; "The Egg and the Chicken," 68–69; "The Foreign Legion," 161–163, 164; *The Hour of the Star*, 135, 137–147, 155–158, 171–172, 176–181; "The Imitation of the Rose," 72–75; lispectorange reading, 61; "Mineirinho," 169; *The Passion According to G.H.*, 59, 69, 71, 75, 76, 77, 115, 134–135, 163–164, 169–171, 178; *The Stream of Life*, 60, 69, 70, 75, 76, 77, 169; "Such Gentleness," 113, 166–169; "Vengeance and Painful Reconciliation," 169
Little red riding hoods, 21
Logos, 15

Madness, 5–6, 32, 35, 89, 113, 143; mad patience, 163; mad purity, 127; mad speed, 111; mad strength, 165; madwomen, 6
Mallarmé, Stéphane: "*Brise Marine*," 24

Mandelstam, Osip, 148
Manet, Julie, 110
Masculine, 25, 142–143, 147, 178; author, 180; relationship to pleasure, 150
Masculinity, 143, 174
Media, 144; mass-mediatized, 62, 146
Metaphor, 2, 20, 50, 114, 156, 170
Monet, Claude, 104–106, 108–113, 120, 123, 129–130
Morewoman, 55
Mozart, Wolfgang Amadeus, 12, 83, 97
Myth, 15

Nationality, 7, 15–16, 47; Africa, 11; America, 108; Brazil, 107; Brazilian, 59, 169, 179; French, 16, 46; German, 132; Japanese, 68, 111, 112; Polish, 99; Ukraine, 132, 179

Other, the, 6, 39, 43, 51, 62, 63, 78, 80, 134, 169, 170, 171; capacity for, 155; difference of, 177; the most, 141, 142; science of the, 66; voice as, 4; the-woman-and-, 71

Papamama, 46
Paradise, 78, 174, 178; Land that is always promised, 41; losers of, 13; Promised Land, 176; rejection of, 4
Passion, 9, 18, 22, 60, 76, 95, 133, 137, 163; according to C.L., 59, 69; according to her, 59; according to the Living, 70; according to Rembrandt, 115; as impassion, 171; of the painter, 108, 109
Penthesilea, 173
Peoples, 41, 46, 48, 55
Percival, 110, 149, 152–154, 174
Political: approach, 62; battles, 53; signs, 45; text, 178

Reading, 13, 23–24, 48, 52, 60, 78, 111, 152, 160; bodily, 52; book of flesh, 175; to clear the gaze, 115; Eve, 151; with eyes closed, 35; the face, 2; the flesh, 26, 42; as gathering, 61; by light of flowers, 72; to live, 20; by love, 43; by media, 65; by her passion, 60; the printed body, 23; reader, 154, 177; without right, 12; what is called, 59; and woman's gaze, 51; writing elects through, 75

Rembrandt, 115, 116, 118–120, 121, 122, 124–126

Rilke, Rainer Maria, 60, 74–75, 132; *The Notebooks of Malte Laurids Brigge*, 73

Rimbaud, Arthur, 115, 132, 148

Rossini, Gioacchino, 80–81, 83, 87, 97, 101, 102; *Tancredi*, 80–103, 147–148, 174–175

Sexuality, 57; without God, 89

Shakespeare, William, 12, 122; King Lear, 122; Lady Macbeth, 122; Romeo and Juliet, 25; Shylock, 122; *Twelfth Night*, 86

Signature: abandoning, 127; of Clarice Lispector, 139; false, 46; of flesh, 53

Signs, 1, 2; fixed, 38, 145; without history, 76; of love, 45; machine of, 52; political and cultural, 45; rose, 73; signifier, 56

Snow White, 19

Soul, 2, 7, 38, 46, 90, 92, 93, 122; body as, 79; body of, 70; "free-soul zone," 98; "hand full of," 64; human, 122; lay of, 54; maternal loversoul, 22; mimosa-soul, 107; paper soulmates, 29; and poverty and wealth, 178; reality of, 127; reeducation of, 134; in silence, 3; soul-attention, 69; soul-ring of lead, 113;

and vision, 4; wellsprings of, 10; and woman, 175

Sphinx, 15

Superuncle, 8, 33, 34

Sutherland, Joan, 86, 93

Tabernacle: breast as, 52

Tasso, Torquato, 78; *Jerusalem Delivered*, 78–103, 172–174, 175

Tom Thumb, 34

Tongue, 4, 21, 22, 25, 45, 52, 55, 58, 148; castrated, 98; dream tongue, 148; French, 32; mother tongue, 21, 28; night tongue, 33; object-tongue, 22

Torah: lungs like scrolls of, 52

Trance: of presence, 73; to go into a *trans*, 84

Tristan and Isolde, 5, 25

Truth, 29, 76, 78, 119, 134, 144, 147, 179; author in, 145–146, 173, 176, 178, 180; Clarice Lispector in, 146, 180; is false, 150; forced, 99, 100; of love, 98, 174; mother in, 180; of mystery, 83; between parentheses, 157; in reserve, 146; voyagers of, 123; and woman, 146, 175

Tsvetaeva, Marina, 148

Unconscious, 45, 56, 58, 80; conscious of, 100; feminine singular, 55; honey of, 21; wild, 152; worldwide, 47, 48

Van Gogh, Vincent, 108, 111, 114, 122, 128

War, 24, 29, 51, 53, 78; army of love, 24; with God, 152; holocausts, 17; of love, 92; Nazis, 48; and pleasure, 18; between races, religions, 80

Wolf, 15, 19, 34; as ever-unsatiable grandmother, 14; Gramma-r wolf, 21–22; for the other, 122

*Library of Congress Cataloging-in-Publication Data*

Cixous, Hélène, 1937–

"Coming to writing" and other essays / Hélène Cixous; with a
foreword by Susan Rubin Suleiman; edited by Deborah Jenson;
translated by Sarah Cornell . . . [et al.].

p.   cm.

Contents: Coming to writing—Clarice Lispector—Tancredi
continues—The last painting or the portrait of God—By the
light of an apple—The author in truth.

Includes index.

ISBN 0–674–14436–8 (alk. paper)

I. Jenson, Deborah. II. Title.

PQ2663.I9C58   1991

844'.914—dc20

90–26785

CIP